U0119066

科学之光
LIGHT OF SCIENCE

世界因他们而改变

达尔文自传

| 中英双语版 |

[英] 查尔斯·达尔文 著

汪莉雅 黄 群 孙 淼 译

中国科学技术出版社

·北 京·

图书在版编目（CIP）数据

达尔文自传：汉英 /（英）查尔斯·达尔文著；汪莉雅，黄群，孙淼译 . —北京：中国科学技术出版社，2023.5

书名原文：The Autobiography of Charles Darwin

ISBN 978-7-5236-0057-3

Ⅰ.①达… Ⅱ.①查… ②汪… ③黄… ④孙… Ⅲ.①达尔文（Darwin, Charles 1809-1882）- 自传 - 汉、英 Ⅳ.① K835.616.15

中国国家版本馆 CIP 数据核字（2023）第 036157 号

策划编辑	周少敏　郭秋霞　崔家岭
责任编辑	李惠兴　崔家岭
装帧设计	中文天地
责任校对	凌　雪
责任印制	马宇晨

出　　版	中国科学技术出版社
发　　行	中国科学技术出版社有限公司发行部
地　　址	北京市海淀区中关村南大街16号
邮　　编	100081
发行电话	010-62173865
传　　真	010-62173081
网　　址	http://www.cspbooks.com.cn

开　　本	787mm×1092mm　1/32
字　　数	143千字
印　　张	7.625
版　　次	2023年5月第1版
印　　次	2023年5月第1次印刷
印　　刷	北京长宁印刷有限公司
书　　号	ISBN 978-7-5236-0057-3 / K·349
定　　价	58.00元

目 录

第1章 开 篇 / 001

第2章 剑桥求学 / 027

第3章 "小猎犬"号的航行 / 046

第4章 回到英国至走向婚姻 / 058

第5章 在伦敦 / 063

第6章 唐恩村的生活 / 076

第7章 《物种起源》及其他作品 / 078

第8章 研究方法总结 / 103

达尔文生平年表 / 116

译者后记 / 117

Contents

Chapter 1 The Beginning / 127

Chapter 2 Cambridge, 1828–1831 / 152

Chapter 3 Voyage of the "Beagle" from Dec. 27, 1831, to Oct. 2, 1836 / 171

Chapter 4 From My Return to England to My Marriage / 182

Chapter 5 From My Marriage, Jan. 29, 1839 to Settling at Down, Sept.14, 1842 / 186

Chapter 6 Residence at Down from Sept. 14, 1842, to the Present Time, 1876 / 198

Chapter 7 My Several Publications / 200

Chapter 8 Written May 1st, 1881 / 223

说　明

　　说来你可能不信，在本书中，我父亲的自传体回忆录是为他的孩子们写的，而且写的时候根本没有想到会出版。但那些了解我父亲的人会明白这样做合情合理。这部自传完整版的标题是"我的思想和性格的发展回忆录"，结尾这样写道："1876 年 8 月 3 日。这本关于我生活的速写大约始于今年的 5 月 28 日，在霍普登（亨斯利·韦奇伍德先生在英国萨里郡的家），从那以后，我几乎每个下午都要写将近一个小时。"他给妻子和孩子所写的私人亲密的记叙，那些段落会在本书中删略。我认为没有必要指出这些删略的地方，相信这也情有可原。书中明显的语言错误已进行了必要的修正，改动的数量已被控制在最低限度。

——弗朗西斯·达尔文

第1章

开　篇

　　一位德国编辑写信给我，让我写自传介绍我的思想和性格的发展。我觉得这种尝试会让我开心，也许会使我的孩子或孩子的孩子感兴趣。如果我能读到我的祖父亲笔所写的思想集——他的所思所想、所作所为以及他是如何工作的，哪怕是简短枯燥，我也会非常感兴趣。接下来我将自述生平，将自己想象成超脱的逝者回顾自己的生活。我也不觉得这有什么困难，因为我已进入暮年，对自己的写作风格毫不在意。

　　我于1809年2月12日出生在英格兰什罗普郡什鲁斯伯里，我最早的记忆只能追溯到我四岁零几个月的时候，那时我们去威尔士阿贝尔格莱附近洗海水浴，我对那里的一些事情和地方有些模糊的记忆。

　　我的母亲①于1817年7月与世长辞，当时我才八岁

---

* 原书本章无章名，现章名是译者为阅读方便所加。

① 苏珊娜·韦奇伍德（1765—1817），约西亚·韦奇伍德一世的长女。

多一点儿。奇怪的是，除了她的病榻、她的黑天鹅绒长袍和她那构造奇特的针线收纳桌，我几乎什么都不记得了。同年春天，我被送到什鲁斯伯里的一所走读学校，在那里待了一年。有人告诉我，我学得比我妹妹凯瑟琳慢得多，我认为我在很多方面都是一个淘气的孩子。

在我上这所走读学校的时候，[这所学校由高街上帝一位论① 教堂的 G. 凯斯牧师开办。达尔文夫人是上帝一位论派教徒，常去凯斯先生的教堂做礼拜，我父亲小时候和他的姐姐们也常去那里。但是，他和他的哥哥都接受了洗礼，打算加入英国国教②。在度过他童年生活的早期之后，他似乎通常都去国教教堂，而不是去凯斯先生的教堂。而现在，小教堂更名"自由基督教会③"，里面竖起了一块壁画碑来纪念我父亲（《圣詹姆斯公报》，

---

① 上帝一位论（Unitarianism）教派，或称"一神论教派"，是欧洲宗教改革时期反对"三位一体"的新教产物，该概念最早形成于 16 世纪后期在波兰－立陶宛和特兰西瓦尼亚。19 世纪英国的上帝一位论教会的会众规模相对较小，受过良好的教育，在达尔文时期比英国国教更允许信仰差异（和怀疑）。

② 英国国教会（Church of England），或称英国圣公会，最早可以追溯到公元 3 世纪在罗马不列颠存在的基督教会，后脱胎于罗马天主教，597 年有了第一任坎特伯雷大主教，最高总督为英国的国王和女王。

③ 20 世纪以后，英国的上帝一位论教派与多教派合并，多使用"自由基督教会"这一更具包容性的命名。

1883 年 12 月 15 日）——弗朗西斯·达尔文注〕我对博物学，尤其是对收藏的兴趣，已经得到了很好的发展。我试图辨别植物的名称。（W. A. 雷顿牧师[1]，我父亲在凯斯先生的学校的校友，他记得有一次我父亲带了一朵花到学校，说母亲教他如何通过观察花的内部识别植物的名称。雷顿先生继续说道："这极大地引起了我的注意和好奇心，我反复地问他这是怎么做到的？"但他的这门学问自然而然还没法传播。——弗朗西斯·达尔文注）我收集了各种各样的东西：贝壳、火漆封章、邮戳、硬币和小矿石。如果收藏的热情能让一个人变成系统的博物学家、艺术家和守财奴，那么这种热情在我身上体现得淋漓尽致，而且显然是天生的，因为我的兄弟姐妹都没有这种兴趣。

　　在入学的那一年，有一件小事深深印在了我的脑海里，我之所以记得如此清楚，是因为从那件事之后我的良心受到了极大的折磨（但愿如此）。诚然不可思议，我在那么小的年龄就对植物的多样性很感兴趣！我告诉另一个小男孩（我记得那是雷顿，他后来成了一位著名的地衣学家和植物学家），我可以用有颜色的液体浇灌出不同色彩

---

[1]　威廉·奥尔波特·雷顿（1805—1889），英国国教牧师、植物学家和编辑。著有《什罗普郡植物志》和《英国地衣植物群》。

的杂交报春[1]和欧报春[2]，这当然是一个无稽谎言，并且我从来没有尝试过。在此，我还得承认，当我还是个小男孩的时候，我就喜欢故意编造一些谎言，而且总是为了引起轰动而这样做。比如有一次，我从父亲的树上采摘了许多珍贵的水果，并把它们藏在灌木丛中，然后上气不接下气地跑去告诉大家我发现了一大堆被偷的水果。

当我第一次来到这所学校的时候，我一定是一个非常单纯的小家伙。学校里有一个叫加内特的男孩有一天带我进了一家蛋糕店，买了一些蛋糕，但他没有付钱，因为店主信任他。我们出来后，我问他为什么不付钱，他立刻回答说："为什么，你不知道我的叔叔在镇上留下了大笔钱？镇上每个商人只要看见戴着我叔叔那顶旧帽子，用特别的姿势扶帽子的人，他们都会免单。"然后他向我展示了他是如何拿走东西。他走进另一家他被信任的商店，要求买一些小东西，他把帽子挪了挪，没有付钱就买到了。我们出来后，他说："现在，如果你想一个人去那家蛋糕店的话（它的确切位置我记得很清楚），我可以把我的帽子借给你。如果你把帽子戴在头上按适

---

① 英国植物学家和园丁菲利普·米勒（1691—1771）通过黄花九轮草与欧报春这两种报春的杂交品种，英文是"polyanthuses"。

② 欧报春，也叫欧洲报春、英国报春、西洋樱草等。

当的方式挪动，你想买什么就可以买什么。"我欣然接受了他慷慨的提议，并进去要了一些蛋糕，整了整这顶旧帽子走出商店。当店主气势汹汹地向我冲来时，我扔下蛋糕狠命逃跑，惊讶地发现加内特这个骗子朋友正冲我哈哈大笑。

就我自己而言，我可以说我小时候是很善良的，但这完全归功于我姐姐们的言传身教。我对人性是自然或天生的这一说法深深质疑。我非常喜欢收集鸟蛋，但一般每次只从鸟巢拿一个蛋，除了有一次，我拿了所有的蛋，不是为了它们的价值，而是纯属为了满足虚荣心。

我对垂钓有强烈的爱好，常常在河边或池塘边看流水潺潺，能坐多久便坐多久。在美尔庄园①（查尔斯·达尔文的舅舅约西亚·韦奇伍德二世的宅邸），有人告诉我，可以用盐水杀死蚯蚓，从那天起，我挂上鱼钩的蚯蚓几乎没有活着的，尽管有时会失败。

当我还是个小男孩，在走读学校的时候，或者说在那之前，我做了件很残忍的事。我打了一只小狗，但我相信这也仅仅是为了享受权力的感觉；不过不可

---

① 美尔庄园，其历史可以追溯至 11 世纪，17 世纪形成了现有的大致样貌，韦奇伍德二世去世后庄园两次易主，现为英国二级保护建筑。

达尔文 7 岁时与妹妹凯瑟琳的画像，1816 年由英国女画家爱伦·沙普尔斯绘制。图片版权已进入公有领域

能打得很严重，小狗没有哀嚎，我敢肯定，那地方离住宅很近。这件事让我深感内疚，我记得起确切的"犯罪现场"就说明了这一点；从那之后，我爱狗更深了，之后很长一段时间是酷爱。狗狗们应该知道这一点，因为我很擅长把它们从主人那里吸引过来，跟它们交流感情。

那一年，我清楚地记得在凯斯先生的学校里发生了另外一件事，那就是一个龙骑兵①的葬礼。我很惊讶于我现在还能清楚地记得当时的场景：那匹马，骑兵的靴子和马枪挂在马鞍上，坟墓边上对天鸣枪。这一场景深深地触动了我心中诗意的想象。

1818 年夏天，我进了巴特勒博士②在什鲁斯伯里的一所大点的学校，我在那儿待到 1825 年仲夏，直到我 16 岁，一共 7 年。我所在的这所学校是寄宿制的，因此，我享受了真正的学生生活。但由于学校离家不到一英里③，我经常在每天两次点名之间、晚上锁门之前跑回家。我想，这在许多方面对我都是有利的，这让我维系了对家庭的感情和兴致。我记得在我早期的学校生活中，我经常必须跑得很快才能赶上时间，而作为一个"飞毛腿"，我通常都很成功；但我在心存疑虑的时候，会向上苍虔诚祈祷，我记得很清楚，我把我的成功归功于祈祷，而不是因为我跑得快，而且还总会惊叹于自己身上的天助之力。

---

① 龙骑兵，17 世纪晚期至 18 世纪早期的欧洲军种，是同时接受马术与步兵战斗技巧的训练，以马匹运输、步行战斗的士兵。

② 塞缪尔·巴特勒（1774—1839），英国古典学者和什鲁斯伯里学校的校长，也是一位主教。

③ 1 英里 =1.609344 千米。

我曾听父亲和大姐说，我在很小的时候，就很喜欢独自长时间散步，但我不知道我在想什么。我经常全神贯注于一些事物。一次，在回学校的路上，路过什鲁斯伯里的旧城防建筑的制高点，那里已经被改造成公共人行步道，我从没有护墙的一侧那里摔了下来，那里的高度只有7至8英尺[①]。然而，在这短暂、突然且完全出乎意料的跌落中，我脑海中闪过数量惊人的想法，这似乎与生理学家证实的每个想法都需要相当多的时间几乎不一致。

对我的思想发展来说，没有什么比巴特勒博士的学校更糟的了，因为那所学校是严格的古典主义学校，除了教一点古代地理和历史，没有教别的东西。学校作为一种教育手段，对我来说简直就是一片空白。我明显从未擅长语言。我花过精力作诗，但这方面我总是做不好。我让许多朋友收集了很多古诗，把这些古诗拼凑起来，有时再加上其他男孩的帮助，这样我就能作出任何主题的诗歌了。我非常注重复习前一天的课程；早晨做礼拜时，我能学会四五十行维吉尔[②]

---

① 大约2.2至2.4米之间。1英尺 =0.3048米。
② 维吉尔（公元前70年—前19年），古罗马诗人，代表作有拉丁语诗集《牧歌集》《农事诗》和史诗《埃涅阿斯纪》。

或荷马[①]的诗，这对我来说轻而易举。但是这个完全没用，因为过了 48 小时后，我会忘记每一节诗。除了作诗，我并不懒散，一般我都是兢兢业业地钻研古典文学，从不打小抄。我诗歌学习中的唯一乐趣，来自贺拉斯[②]的一些颂诗，因为我非常欣赏。

当我离开这所学校的时候，就我的年龄来说，我的成绩既不好也不坏。我相信我所有的老师和我的父亲都认为我是一个非常普通的孩子，智力低于一般标准的那种。令我深感屈辱的是，父亲曾对我说："你只知道打猎、玩狗和捉老鼠，将来不仅一事无成，还会让你的家人蒙羞。"我的父亲[③]是我所认识的最善良的人，我也衷心地怀念他，但当他说那些话时，他一定出于生气，才有失偏颇。

我尽可能地回顾我在寄宿学校的性格，在这一时

---

① 荷马（约公元前 9 世纪—前 8 世纪），相传为古希腊失明的吟游诗人，代表作有古希腊语史诗《伊利亚特》和《奥德赛》，两者统称《荷马史诗》。目前没有确切证据证明荷马的存在，所以也有人认为他是传说中被构造出来的人物。

② 昆图斯·贺拉斯·弗拉库斯（公元前 65 年—前 8 年），罗马帝国奥古斯都时期著名诗人、批评家、翻译家，代表作有《颂诗》。他和维吉尔、奥维德并称古罗马三大诗人。

③ 罗伯特·达尔文（1766—1848），英国著名外科医师，"微眼跳"研究的先驱人物。

期，唯一让我有前途的品质，是我强烈而多样化的兴趣，对任何让我感兴趣的东西都充满热情，对理解任何复杂的难题或事物都有极度的快感。一位私人教师教我欧几里得几何学[1]，我清楚地记得几何证明给我带来了强烈的满足感。我同样清楚地记得我的姑父[2]（弗朗西斯·高尔顿[3]的父亲）给我的快乐，他解释了气压计游标的原理。我兴趣广泛，除科学之外，我喜欢读各种各样的书，我过去常常花数小时读莎士比亚的历史剧，通常是坐在学校厚墙的一扇旧窗边。我还读过其他诗歌，比如詹姆斯·汤姆森[4]的《四季》，以及拜伦[5]和司各特[6]最近出版的诗歌。我之所以提到这一点，是因为在我晚年，我完全失去了对所有诗歌的兴趣，包括莎士比亚

---

① 欧几里得（公元前 325 年—前 265 年），古希腊数学家，被称为"几何学之父"。他在著作《几何原本》中提出五大公设，在欧洲自 1482 年第一次印刷以来出版的版本数量仅次于圣经。后文将其简称为"欧式几何"。

② 塞缪尔·特提乌斯·高尔顿（1783—1844），商人和科学家。

③ 弗朗西斯·高尔顿（1822—1911），英国著名生物学家、统计学家和探险家，"优生学"和"高尔顿钉版"模型的创始人。

④ 詹姆斯·汤姆森（1700—1748），苏格兰诗人兼剧作家，著名诗歌有《四季》和《惰性城堡》。

⑤ 乔治·戈登·拜伦，第六代拜伦男爵（1788—1824），简称拜伦勋爵，是一位英国诗人。浪漫主义文学运动的主要人物之一，代表作有长篇叙事诗《唐璜》和《柴尔德哈罗德的朝圣》。

⑥ 沃尔特·司各特爵士（1771—1832），苏格兰历史小说家、诗人、剧作家和历史学家。代表作《撒克逊英雄传》。

的，我深感遗憾。关于诗歌意境带来的乐趣，我还想补充一点，1822 年在威尔士边境的一次骑马旅行第一次激活了我头脑中欣赏风景所感受到的生动喜悦，这种喜悦是那么地持久，超过了所有其他事物带给我的审美快感。

在我早期的上学时光，一个男孩有一本《世界奇观》①，我经常阅读，并与其他男孩争论其中一些陈述的真实性；我相信这本书让我萌生了去偏远国家旅行的想法，而"小猎犬"号皇家军舰的航行最终实现了这个愿望。在学校生活的后半段，我变得热衷于射击；我相信，没有人比我对猎鸟的热情更高的了。我清楚地记得我打死的第一只沙锥鸟，我太兴奋了，以至于手抖到很难给枪上膛。这种兴趣持续了很长时间，让我成了一个很好的猎手。到后来在剑桥的时候，我经常在镜子前练习托枪过肩，看着自己把枪端得很正。另一个更好的练习方案是让一个朋友举着点燃的蜡烛，摆动手臂使火苗在一个方向，然后我把枪的火帽套在火门上，不上膛直接击发，瞄得准的话，一小股气流就会把蜡烛吹

---

① 这本书有可能是 1740 年英国奥克利教区牧师长 G. 纳尔逊主编的《世界自然奇观展》(*The Wonders of Nature Throughout the World Display'd*)。

灭。火帽的爆破发出尖锐的声音，之后我听说，学院的助教说："达尔文同学似乎花几个小时在他的房间里抽马鞭，多么惊人，我每次从他窗边路过都能听见屋里噼啪作响。"

我在学生时代有许多至亲至爱的朋友，我想我那时是个感情丰富的人。

在科学方面，我继续以极大的热情收集矿物，但这种热情很不科学——我只关心新命名的矿物，但几乎没有对它们进行分类。我当时观察昆虫一定是小心翼翼地，我 10 岁时（1819 年）在威尔士的普拉斯爱德华兹海滩待了三个星期，我看见过一种大型黑红相间的半翅目[①]昆虫、许多飞蛾（斑蛾属[②]）以及在什罗普郡没有见过的一种虎甲属[③]昆虫，感到又惊又喜。我几乎下定决心开始收集所有我能发现的死昆虫，因为在和我二姐商量之后，我得出结论，为了收集昆虫而杀生是不对的。

---

① 半翅目（*Hemiptera*）是昆虫纲下的一目，1758 年由瑞典动植物分类学家卡尔·林奈（1707—1778）命名。

② 斑蛾属（*Zygaena*）目前暂无官方中文属名，直译为斑蛾属是昆虫纲鳞翅目斑蛾科下的一属，1775 年由林奈的学生约翰·克里斯蒂安·法布里修斯（1745—1808）命名。

③ 虎甲属（*Cicindela*）是昆虫纲鞘翅目虎甲科下的一属，1758 年由林奈命名。

读了吉尔伯特·怀特[①]的《塞尔伯恩博物志》后，我很喜欢观察鸟类的习性，甚至还为此做了笔记。在我单纯的想法中，我记得自己想知道为什么不是每个绅士都能成为一个鸟类学家。

　　我在这所寄宿学校的生活接近尾声时，我的哥哥[②]努力地学习化学，并适当地用工具室里的器械在花园里的建造了一个很好的实验室，我还被允许在他的大部分实验中充当助手。他制造了各种的气体和许多化合物。我非常仔细地阅读了几本化学书籍，如亨利和帕克斯的《化学教理问答》(*Chemical Catechism*)[③]。我对这门学科很感兴趣，我和哥哥经常忙碌到深夜。这是我在学校教育中最大的收获，因为它让我从实践中明白了实验科学的意义。我们研究化学的事在学校里不知怎么就被人知道了，由于这样的事情前所未有，我获得了"毒气"这个绰号。我还曾被校长巴特勒博士当众斥责，因为我把时间浪费在这些无用的学科上：他给了我一个很不公正

① 　吉尔伯特·怀特（1720—1793）是一位英国博物学家、生态学家和鸟类学家的先驱。其作品《塞尔伯恩博物志》自出版后一直享有良好的口碑。
② 　伊拉斯谟·阿尔维·达尔文（1804—1881），罗伯特·达尔文长子，在爱丁堡大学完成医学学习，后于1829年病退，尔后还保持了一段时间的社会活跃度。
③ 　此处指英国化学家塞缪尔·帕克斯（1761—1825）的《化学教理问答》，此处的亨利有可能是同时期化学家威廉·亨利（1774—1836）。

的评价——"poco curante"①，我不明白他的意思，但我觉得这是一种可怕的责备。

父亲很明智，由于我在学校成绩不好，他在我毕业之前就带我走了，并把我送到爱丁堡大学和我哥哥一起（1825年10月）②，在那里我待了两（学）年。我的哥哥快要完成他的医学学习了，虽然我感觉他从来没有真正打算从医，而我是被送到那儿准备学医。学了一段时间后，我从各种小事中意识到，我父亲会留给我足够维持舒适安逸生活的财产，尽管我从来没有想过我会成为这么富有的人，但我的想法动摇了我刻苦学医的决心。

爱丁堡大学的教学完全由讲座课组成，除了霍普教授③的化学课，其他都枯燥得令人难以忍受。在我看来，与阅读相比，上课不仅没有好处，反而有很多缺点。邓肯医生在冬天早晨8点的药物学讲座课让我想起来就觉得可怕。××博士④关于人体解剖学的讲座就像他自己一

_____

① 法国启蒙思想家伏尔泰通过意大利语创造的一个词，意思是"无动于衷之人"。

② 此处的爱丁堡大学是指爱丁堡大学医学院，据史料显示该学院为当时英国数一数二的医学院，查尔斯·达尔文的父亲和爷爷都毕业于此。查尔斯去到爱丁堡大学时年仅16岁，1827年4月离校。

③ 托马斯·查尔斯·霍普（1766—1844），英国医生、化学家和讲师。他证明了元素锶的存在，并证明水在4℃时达到最大密度。

④ 此处为弗朗西斯·达尔文对原手稿的删略。

样枯燥乏味，这门课的主题令我厌恶。可后来才发现，我一生中最大的罪恶之一便是没有鼓励自己去练习解剖，如果我很快克服了厌恶，之后的实践对我未来的工作将是无价的。这是一种无法挽回的罪恶，就像我没能学会绘画一样。我还定期去医院的临床病房见习，其中一些病例使我十分痛苦，一些画面至今仍历历在目；但幸亏我还没有傻到因为厌恶而减少出勤。我真不理解为什么我对医学课程这一部分没有更多的兴趣；在返校前的那个夏天我开始在什鲁斯伯里给一些弱势群体看病，主要是妇女和儿童，我尽可能详细地写下了病例的所有症状，然后大声读给我父亲听，而他会提议做进一步的诊断，并建议我用什么药物，让我自行调配。有一次，我接诊了至少12个病人，并对这份工作产生了浓厚的兴趣。我的父亲是我所认识的最能判断人的个性的人，他断言我将成为一名成功的医生，病人都爱找的那种。他坚持认为，自我激励是成功的主要因素；但他在我身上所看到的，使他相信我应该建立我自己都不知道的信心。我还在爱丁堡的医院观摩过两次手术，又亲眼见到了两例非常糟糕的手术，其中一次是在一个孩子身上，但我在手术完成之前就匆匆离开了。我也没有再次参加，因为没有足够强大的理由让我这么去做，这距离氯仿（麻醉剂）问世的神圣之日还有很长一段时间。而这两个可怕的手术在我的心头萦绕了多年。

我只和我哥哥同校了一年，在第二年，我就全靠自己了；这是一个有利条件，因为我结识了几个喜欢博物学的年轻人。其中之一是安斯沃思，他后来出版了他的《亚述游记》①；他是一位维尔纳博物学会②的地质学家，对许多学科都略知一二。科尔德斯特里姆博士③是一个完全不同的年轻人，他拘谨、稳重、高度虔诚，心肠也很好，后来发表了几篇很好的动物学文章。第三个年轻人是哈迪④，我想，他本可以成为一名

---

① 威廉·弗朗西斯·安斯沃思（1807—1896）是英国外科医生、旅行家、地理学家和地质学家，还当过作家和编辑，该游记全名为《对亚述、巴比伦和卡尔迪亚的考察》(*Researches in Assyria，Babylonia，and Chaldæa*)。

② 维尔纳博物学会（1808—1858年）是爱丁堡大学一个对博物学广泛涉猎的学术团体，也是当时爱丁堡皇家学会的一个分支，进行有关矿物学、植物、昆虫的学术考察。学会名字源于德国地质学家亚伯拉罕·戈特洛布·维尔纳，地质学"水成论"的提出人，也是学会创始人罗伯特·詹姆逊的老师。

③ 约翰·科尔德斯特里姆（1806—1863）苏格兰医生，达尔文的挚友。

④ 詹姆斯·哈迪（1802—1844），据史料显示为博士和地质学家，最初研究数学、化学和博物学，爱丁堡植物学会会员。1822年在爱丁堡大学医学院毕业后在印度军队中担任了一系列职位。

优秀的植物学家，但他很早就在印度去世了。最后是格兰特博士[①]，比我年长几岁，但我不记得我是如何认识他的；他发表了一些一流的动物学论文，但是，他来到伦敦以后，作为大学学院的教授，在科学方面再没有做过什么，这是我一直无法理解的事实。我很了解他，他态度冷淡，拘谨的外表下，却充满了热情。有一天，我们在一起散步时，他突然对拉马克[②]和他的进化论赞不绝口。我吃惊而又默默地听着，这是我所能判断的，但对我的思想没有任何影响。我以前读过我爷爷的《动物生理学》[③]，书中也保留了类似的观点，但对我没有产生任何影响。然而，很可能是因为早期就听到这种观点被支持和赞扬，才助我日后在《物种起源》中以另一种形式坚持这些观点。这时，我非常钦佩《动物生理学》，但隔了十年至十五年再读一遍

① 罗伯特·埃德蒙·格兰特（1793—1874），英国解剖学家和动物学家，与达尔文家族在学术上有一定交集。

② 让-巴蒂斯特·拉马克（1744—1829），法国博物学家，生物进化学说的伟大奠基人之一。1809年发表的《动物哲学》中提出了"用进废退"与"获得性遗传"两个法则，强调了生物适应环境所产生的进化，其进化思想在达尔文生活的早期占据一定社会地位，但其严谨性受到质疑。

③ 《动物生理学；或有机生命法则》（*Zoonomia；or the Laws of Organic Life*），作者是达尔文的爷爷伊拉斯谟·达尔文医生（1730—1795），分两卷，涉及病理学、解剖学、心理学和身体机能。

时，我感到非常失望。推测的比例太大，事实呈现却很少。

格兰特博士和科尔德斯特里姆博士非常关注海洋动物学，我经常陪同格兰特博士在潮池中收集动物，我尽可能仔细地解剖了这些动物。我还与纽黑文镇的一些渔民成了朋友，和他们一起用拖网捕捞牡蛎，因此获得了许多标本。但是由于没有经过任何常规的解剖练习，并且只有一个小破显微镜，我的尝试非常失败。尽管如此，我还是收获了一个有趣的小发现，并于1826年初在普林尼学会[①]的成员面前朗读了我写的这个主题短文。文章中提到所谓藻苔虫属（*Flustra*）[②]的卵细胞借助纤毛实现独立运动的能力，实际上是幼虫。在另一篇短文中，我展示了那些原本被认为是 *Fucus loreus*[③] 幼年状态

---

① 普林尼学会（1823—1841年）是爱丁堡大学的一个博物学学生俱乐部。命名源自古罗马海军司令、自然学家普林尼。由约翰·贝尔德三兄弟发起。学会以唯物主义的观点挑战了正统的宗教科学观念。最初的成员包括约翰·科尔德斯特里姆、詹姆斯·哈迪和罗伯特·格兰特。

② 藻苔虫属（*Flustra*）是苔藓动物门、裸唇纲、唇口目、藻苔虫科下的一属，1758年及1761年由林奈命名。

③ *Fucus loreus* 系生物属种名，1767年由林奈命名，之后属种改作"*Himanthalia elongata*"，由专攻藻类的丹麦牧师和植物学家汉斯·克里斯蒂安·林格拜（1782—1837）定义属，为褐藻门、褐藻纲、墨角藻目"*Himanthaliaceae*"科唯一属种，在英文里有"thongweed""sea thong""sea spaghetti"几个俗名，可叫"细绳海草"。

的球状小体，其实是 *Pontobdella muricata*[①] 的卵囊。

我相信对普林尼学会的支持是由罗伯特·詹姆逊教授所发起的[②]。学会由学生组成，在大学的一间地下室里聚会，阅读有关博物学的论文并进行讨论。我过去经常参加这些聚会，这激发了我的热情，让我结交了志趣相投的新朋友，对我产生了很好的影响。一天晚上，一个可怜的年轻人站起身起来，结巴了很长时间，脸涨得通红，终于慢慢地说出了这句话："会长，我忘了我要说什么。"这个可怜的家伙看起来不知所措，所有的成员都非常惊讶，以至于没有人能想出一个词来掩盖他的困窘。我们这个小团体里宣读的文章都没有印刷，所以我没享受到我的文章印刷出来的满足感；但我看格兰特博士在他优秀的藻苔虫属学术论文中注意到了我的小发现[③]。

---

① *Pontobdella muricata* 系生物属种名，属于环节动物门、环带纲、吻蛭目、鱼蛭科下的属种，1758 年由林奈命名，是一种表面多刺形突起的海蛭，有一个俗名"鳐鱼蛭"（skate leech）。
② 罗伯特·詹姆逊为普林尼学会高级荣誉会员，但该学会是否由他直接创立，还存在争议。
③ 1827 年 7 月，格兰特在《爱丁堡科学杂志》上发表了一篇关于藻苔虫属的卵和海蛭卵的文章［Grant, R. E. 1827. Notice regarding the ova of the Pontobdella muricata, Lam. Edinburgh Journal of Science 7（1）：160–161.］，致谢中有"首先确定它们属于这种生物的功劳要归于我热心的年轻朋友、什鲁斯伯里的查尔斯·达尔文先生"，这也是达尔文的名字第一次出现在印刷物上。

我当时也是英国皇家医学会的一员，并且经常参加学会的活动；但由于他们主题只有医学，我对他们不算太关注。学会里面有一些毫无用处的演讲，但也不乏好的演讲者，在我看来最好的是后来的 J. 凯－沙特尔沃思爵士[①]。格兰特博士偶尔带我去参加维尔纳博物学会的会议，会上阅读、讨论各种博物学的论文，然后发表在《学报》[②]上。我听到奥杜邦[③]在那里发表了一些关于北美鸟类习性的有趣论述，不公正地嘲笑了沃特顿[④]。顺便说一句，我认识一个黑人，住在爱丁堡，他跟随沃特顿一起旅行，并以制作鸟类标本，主要是以剥制和填充技艺为生，他技艺精湛，还给我有偿授课，他是一个非常有趣和聪明的人，我过去常常和他坐在一

---

① 詹姆斯·菲利普斯·凯－沙特尔沃思爵士，第一代准男爵（1804—1877），英国政治家和教育家。他创办过的一所继续教育学院最终成为圣马可和圣约翰大学。

② 此处的《学报》有可能是维尔纳博物学会的内部刊物《维尔纳博物学会回忆录》（*Memoirs of the Wernerian Natural History Society*），也可能是《爱丁堡哲学杂志》（*Edinburgh Philosophical Journal*），还可能是收录在《爱丁堡皇家学会学报》（*Transactions of the Royal Society of Edinburgh*）里。

③ 约翰·詹姆斯·奥杜邦（1785—1851），法裔美国画家、博物学家，他绘制的鸟类图鉴《美国鸟类》被称作"美国国宝"。

④ 查尔斯·沃特顿（1782—1865），英国博物学家、种植园监督员和探险家，以其在自然保护方面的开创性工作而闻名。

块儿①。

......

莱纳德·霍纳②先生还带我参加了一次爱丁堡皇家学会③的会议，我在会上看到沃尔特·司各特④爵士担任主席，他向与会各方表示歉意，说自己人微望轻，难任斯职。我怀着赞叹和崇敬之心看着他和全场，我想正是由于我年轻时的那次参会，以及当年在皇家医学会的参与，在我几年前被选为这两个学会的荣誉会员时，我认为这比其他任何同类荣誉都意义重大。如果当年有人告诉我，有一天我会得到这样的荣誉，我一定会说这是不可能发生的荒唐事，就像有人告诉你，你要当选英国国王一样。

在爱丁堡的第二年，我参加了××教授⑤的地质学和动物学的课，但它们令人难以置信地枯燥。它们对我产生的唯一影响是，只要我活着，就决不会读地质学方

---

① 达尔文提到的这位黑人标本制作师，史料显示，为约翰·爱德蒙斯顿（生卒年不详），出生时为南美英属圭亚那的非洲奴隶，曾陪同沃特顿在南美考察，后随白人奴隶主来到英国并熟练掌握标本制作，也是查尔斯·达尔文在学习标本制作的重要导师。

② 莱纳德·霍纳（1785—1864），苏格兰商人、地质学家和教育改革家。

③ 爱丁堡皇家学会（1783年至今），是从爱丁堡医学会分出来的致力于更为广阔的科学门类的组织。

④ 前文提到达尔文读到的、和拜伦同时期的诗人。

⑤ 此处为弗朗西斯·达尔文对原手稿的删略。

面的书，或以任何方式研究这门科学。其实我当初已经准备好对这一主题进行严肃的探讨；在当初的两三年前，什罗普郡有一位对岩石非常了解的科顿老先生曾向我指出，什鲁斯伯里的镇上那块著名的漂砾，叫作"钟石"；他告诉我，在坎伯兰郡或苏格兰附近都没有类似岩石，并郑重保证，世界末日来临前，都不会有人能够解释这块石头是如何来到这里的。这给我留下了深刻的印象，我时常静静思考这块神奇的石头。因此，当我第一次读到冰山在运送巨石方面的作用时，我感受到了最强烈的喜悦，我为地质学的进步而自豪。还有一件事也给我留下了深刻的印象，尽管我现在只有 67 岁，还不够老：在索尔兹伯里峭壁[1]的一次野外课上，教授站在一块暗色岩脉上，岩石的地层都硬化了，边缘还有杏仁状气泡孔隙，我们周围都是火山岩，教授却说这岩石裂缝上的沉积层是在上面积累形成的，还冷笑道：居然有人坚持认为沉积层是裂缝下面熔岩注入的。[2]有这样的经历，就不难解释我

---

[1] 索尔兹伯里峭壁（Salisbury Crags）位于英国苏格兰首都爱丁堡荷里路德公园（Holyrood Park）内的西边，系一组约 46 米高的悬崖。

[2] 此段为地质学"水成论"（亚伯拉罕·戈特洛布·维尔纳提出，维尔纳学派提倡）的主张，即地球上的岩石都是在水中沉积形成的，不承认存在火成岩一类的岩石。而当时已经有科学家提出与之相对的"火成论"，即岩石是由地下热能及火山活动所改变的。

当时为什么决定永远不会专注地质学了。

在参加××的讲座时，我结识了博物馆馆长麦吉利夫雷先生[①]，他后来出版了一本关于苏格兰鸟类的大型优秀书籍。我和他进行了许多有趣的博物学对话，他对我很好。鉴于我当时收集海洋软体动物，他给了我一些稀有的贝壳来鼓励我，可惜那时我还谈不上热忱。

那两年的暑假总归是被我玩掉了，尽管我手里总是拿着一些书，还饶有兴趣地读着。1826年夏天，我和两个朋友背着背包徒步穿越北威尔士。我们每天大致步行30英里，包括登上斯诺登峰的那天。我还和二姐一起去北威尔士骑马旅行，雇了一个仆人带着马鞍包存放我们的衣服。秋天我主要是在欧文先生的伍德豪斯庄园[②]和我舅舅乔斯（约西亚·韦奇伍德二世[③]，伊特鲁里亚工厂创始人[④]的儿子）的美尔庄园打猎。我的热情是如此之高，以至

---

① 威廉·麦吉利夫雷（1796—1852），苏格兰博物学家和鸟类学家。
② 伍德豪斯是位于英格兰什罗普郡西费尔顿的一座乡间别墅，由建筑师罗伯特·麦林为政治家威廉·莫斯汀·欧文于1773—1774年建造。庄园占地1500英亩。现为英国二级保护建筑。
③ 约西亚·韦奇伍德二世（1769—1843），英国企业家，继承其父约西亚·韦奇伍德一世的陶艺公司。1832年至1835年他担任过市议员。
④ 约西亚·韦奇伍德一世（1730—1795），英国陶艺制作师与企业家，伊特鲁里亚工厂是其1769年在英格兰斯塔福德郡特伦特河畔斯托克区开设的一家陶瓷厂，这家工厂经营了180余年。

于我常常在睡觉时把射击靴放在床边，以免在早上穿靴子时浪费半分钟；有一次，我在 8 月 20 日到美尔庄园的一个偏远地方打黑琴鸡①，我和猎场看守人在茂密的石南和新种的欧洲赤松中艰难步行了一天，也没看见一只猎物。

整个狩猎季中，我对射杀的每一只鸟都做了准确的记录。有一天，当我和欧文上尉（庄园主长子）和少校希尔（欧文的堂兄，后来的伯威克勋爵）一起在伍德豪斯打猎。虽然这两人我都很喜欢，但那次我觉得自己被要了，因为每次我开了枪，认为打死了一只鸟，他俩其中一人就会假装给枪上膛，还喊道："这只不算，因为我同时开了枪。"猎场看守员看出他们在开玩笑，就给他们帮腔。几个小时后，他们告诉了我这个玩笑，但这对我来说可不是玩笑，因为我已经射杀了很多只鸟，但不知道有多少只了，也无法将它们添加到我的列表中（我一般都是用一根绑在扣眼上的绳子打结计数）。这两缺德鬼一定是觉察到了这一点。

我当时是多么热衷于射击！但下意识为自己的热情

① 黑琴鸡（学名：*Lyrurus tetrix*）为雉科琴鸡属的鸟类，俗名黑野鸡、黑松鸡等，中国东北地区、河北东北部、内蒙古东北部、新疆北部等地都有分布，黑琴鸡在中国属于保护动物，不允许狩猎。

感到羞愧，因为我在试图让自己相信射击几乎是一种智力劳动，需要很高的技巧来判断在哪里可以找到最多的猎物，并需要很好地训练猎狗。

1827 年秋天对美尔庄园的一次访问令我难忘，因为我在那里见到了 J. 麦金托什爵士①本人，他是我接触过的最好的交谈者。后来，我听到他说："那个年轻人身上有某种让我感兴趣的东西。"这让我感到由衷地自豪。他看出我对他说的每一件事都很感兴趣，毕竟我对历史、政治和道德哲学一概不知。我认为，听到一位知名人士的赞扬，虽然无疑容易或肯定会激起虚荣心，但对一个年轻人来说是有益的，因为这有助于他走上正确的道路。

尔后的两三年里，我对美尔庄园的访问非常愉快，与秋猎无关。那里的生活完全自由；这乡间很适合步行或骑马；晚上，他们会有很多非常愉快的谈话，因为是大型家庭聚会，所以话题不是那么私人化，还伴有音乐。夏天，全家人常常坐在老门廊的台阶上，前面是花园，房子对面陡峭的树林河岸映在湖面上，不时有鱼儿浮出水面，或是有水鸟在水里嬉戏。没有什么比在美尔

① 詹姆斯·麦金托什爵士（1765—1832），苏格兰法学家、辉格党政治家和历史学家。

庄园的这些夜晚在我脑海中留下的画面更生动了。我也非常依恋和尊敬我的舅舅乔斯，他沉默寡言，是个非常有威严的人；但他有时会和我畅所欲言。他是那种正直的人，判断力极强。我不相信地球上有任何力量能让他偏离他认为正确的方向一英寸。我过去常常在脑海中把著名的《贺拉斯颂》用在他身上，现在我已经忘记了，其中有"暴君的威胁"几个字。

（正直坚定的人，

无论是愤怒市民的误解，

还是暴君的威胁，

都不能动摇他坚定的意志。）

第 2 章

剑桥求学

在爱丁堡待了两学年后，我父亲察觉到，或者从我姐姐们那里听到，我不喜欢当医生，所以他建议我去当牧师。他十分强烈地斥责我变成游手好闲只爱运动的人，因为当时我很可能就会变成那样。我要求给我一些时间考虑，基于我的所闻所思，我无法公开宣布我信仰英国国教的所有教义，要不然我还是喜欢当一名乡村牧师的。因此，我认真读了"皮尔森信条"①和其他几本关于神学的书；当时，我对《圣经》中每一条必须严格遵守的刻板事实深信不疑。因此，我很快说服自己完全接受信条。

考虑到我受到过正统教派的猛烈批判②，我曾打算当一名牧师的想法看来还是荒谬的。我当初考虑当牧师，遵从父亲的意愿，而这一想法直到我离开剑桥，加入

---

① 《信条的阐述》（*Exposition of the Creed*），为英国神学者约翰·皮尔森1659 年首次出版的作品，是圣公会使徒信经中最具影响力的著作之一。
② 此处指代之后教会对达尔文的"物种进化论"的批判。

"小猎犬"号成为博物学者时①，才自然消逝。如果颅相学家有公信力，从某一方面来说，我是很适合当牧师的。几年前，德国一个心理学会的秘书们给我写信，恳切地要我寄一张自己的照片；过了一段时间，我收到了一个会议的通知，说是要公开讨论我的颅型，其中一位发言人宣称，我颅骨的凸起是主教的象征，顶得上十名牧师。

由于家里决定让我当一名牧师，我有必要到一所英国的大学去拿个学位。但由于我离开学校后从未打开过一本古典书籍，我沮丧地发现，在这两年里，我几乎把所有学过的还给了老师，甚至忘了一些希腊字母，多么令人难以置信。因此，我没有按照通常的 10 月份去剑桥大学入学②，而是在什鲁斯伯里找了一位家庭教师。1828年年初，圣诞节假期过后，我才去了剑桥大学③。我很快就恢复了上学时的知识水平，能够相当熟练地翻译一些简单的希腊书籍，如《荷马史诗》和希腊语《圣经》④。

---

① 指达尔文从剑桥大学毕业后，于 1831 年登上"小猎犬"号，本书第 3 部分会详细叙述。

② 据史料显示，达尔文没按时入学是因为没有通过考试。

③ 达尔文通过了考试，进入剑桥大学基督学院。

④ 《圣经》的旧约公认是最早用希伯来文写的，而新约大多被认定为是"通用希腊语"（西罗马帝国时期形成的希腊语）所写的，此处指代希腊语新约《圣经》在英国正统天主教派中修订的版本，随着宗教运动的不断推进，英语版本《圣经》的流行超过了希腊语版。

在剑桥的三年里，就学术研究而言，我的时间完全被浪费了，就像在爱丁堡大学和在两所基础教育学校一样。我学数学不精，在1828年夏天和一位家庭教师（一个枯燥的人）去了威尔士的巴茅斯，但学业进展非常缓慢。数学功课竟是如此令我反感，主要也是因为我在代数学习的早期阶段没悟出任何意义。这种不耐烦是非常愚蠢的，多年以后，我一直深感遗憾，因为如此有天赋的数学家们似乎有一种超感知能力，而我没有学得足够多，至少没有理解一些重要的数学原理。但我当时觉得自己应该低分飘过，不用取得更高的成绩。至于古典文学，我什么也没做，只是上了一些大学的必修课程，而且出勤率几乎是低得可怜。第二年，我必须努力一两个月才能通过学士学位初试，终究还是轻松通过了。在最后一年里，为了拿下文学学士学位，我又一次认真起来，捡回了古典文学，还学了一点代数和欧式几何，后者给我带来了很多乐趣，就像在原来的学校时那样。为了通过文学学士考试，还必须学习佩利[1]的"基督教理据"和"伦理学"[2]。我学得很

---

[1] 威廉·佩利（1743—1805），英国牧师、"自然神学"辩护者和实用主义哲学家。在英国启蒙运动晚期发挥重要作用，推动了英国的宗教改革。
[2] 全书名分别为《基督教理据的观点》（*View of the Evidences of Christianity*）和《道德与政治哲学原理》（*The Principles of Moral and Political Philosophy*），当时被选为剑桥大学的课本。

透彻，我相信自己可以全然无误默写出"理据"，但当然不是用佩利那么清晰的语言。我要补充一下，这本书的逻辑，以及他的"自然神学"，给我带来了和学欧式几何一样多的快乐。但我还是觉得，不死记硬背地认真研读这些作品，只是学术课程中的一部分，但对我的思想教育几乎无用，当时我这么觉得，现在仍然如此。毕竟当时我并没有促使自己对佩利的论证前提进行反思，之所以相信这些，是因为我被他一长串的论证迷住了，被说服了。佩利这门课的考试我答得很好，欧式几何也答得挺好，古典文学课也没有掉链子，因而在那些不慕荣誉的人群中取得了一个好名次。说来也怪，我不记得自己的排名，但记得自己在名单上的第 5、第 10 或第 12 个名字之间波动。（1831 年 1 月名单上的第 10 名）

大学里举办过几个学科的公开讲座，都是自愿参加的，但我在爱丁堡已经对讲座感到厌恶，以至于没有去听塞奇威克①有趣而雄辩的讲座。如果去了，我可能

① 亚当·塞奇威克（1785—1873），英国地质学家和英国圣公会牧师，曾任伦敦地质学会会长，现代地质学的奠基人之一，1835 年提出了"寒武纪"这个地质概念，本章及后文将多次出现。

会更早成为一名地质学家。然而，我参加了亨斯洛①的植物学讲座，非常喜欢，因为讲得极其清晰，还配有极其出色的插图。但我没有学植物学。亨斯洛曾经带着他的学生，进行实地考察，步行或坐马车，或乘驳船顺流而下，去到远方，并就所观察到的稀有植物和动物进行教学。这些远足令我愉快。

令我痛心疾首的是，我挥霍了我的剑桥生活，甚至比挥霍还糟，尽管现在我们还能看到我有些试图补救的成分。由于不能射击和狩猎、骑马穿越乡间，我加入了一个运动圈子，结交的不乏一些放荡的年轻人。我们经常在晚上一起吃饭，虽然这类晚餐通常有更高地位的人参加，但并不妨碍我们有时喝得太多，然后愉快地唱歌和打牌。我理应为这样虚度时光而感到羞愧，但是，一些朋友非常令我愉快，大家兴致都很高，所以，每当我回忆起这些日子，我就禁不住感到非常愉快。

回忆起我许多性格截然不同的朋友，我会感到很

① 约翰·亨斯洛（1796—1861），英国牧师、植物学家和地质学家，和剑桥大学塞奇威克等教授一起创立了剑桥哲学学会，本章及后文会讲到他与达尔文的深厚友谊。

开心。我和惠特利[1]（尊者 C. 惠特利，杜伦的教士，以前是杜伦大学自然哲学的高级讲师）关系很好，他后来是剑桥大学荣誉学位考试中级优胜者，我们经常一起散步。他给我灌输了绘画和丰富的雕刻术的品鉴知识，我对其中一些作品非常欣赏并购买收藏。我经常去菲茨威廉的画廊[2]，我当时鉴赏力一定相当不错，因为我所欣赏的一般是最好的画，我和老馆长讨论过这些画。我还饶有兴趣地读了约书亚·雷诺兹爵士[3]的书。这种鉴赏力，虽然不是我与生俱来的，却持续了好几年。伦敦国家美术馆的许多画都给我带来了极大的乐趣，如塞巴斯蒂安·德尔·皮翁博[4]的作品唤起我心中崇高的美感。

我还进入了一个音乐爱好者团体，我相信是通过我的热心朋友赫伯特（已故的约翰·莫里斯·赫伯特，卡迪夫和蒙茅斯巡回法院的县法院法官），他获得过一个剑桥大学荣誉学位考试高级优胜者学位。通过与这些人交往，聆

---

[1] 查尔斯·托马斯·惠特利牧师（1808—1895），英国数学与医学学者，和达尔文一样，先后就读于什鲁斯伯里学校和剑桥大学，曾参与英国杜伦大学的创立。

[2] 画廊隶属于菲茨威廉博物馆，系剑桥大学的艺术和古物博物馆，位于剑桥市中部。1816 年由第七代菲茨威廉子爵的遗赠建造，是西欧最好的古董和现代艺术收藏地之一。

[3] 约书亚·雷诺兹爵士（1723—1792），英国画家，专攻肖像画。

[4] 塞巴斯蒂安·德尔·皮翁博（1485—1547），文艺复兴晚期画家。

听他们的演奏，我对音乐产生了浓厚的兴趣，并经常用音乐为散步计时，这样在工作日也能听到国王学院教堂的圣歌了。这给我带来了强烈的快感，以至于我的脊梁有时会颤抖。我敢肯定我的这门爱好里没有矫饰或纯粹的模仿，因为我通常一个人上国王学院，有时还请唱诗班的男孩在我的房间里唱歌。然而，我耳力完全不好，乐感不佳，以至于察觉不到不和谐，不能把握时间，也不能唱准一支曲子；我是如何从音乐中获得快乐的，这是一个谜。

我音乐界的朋友们很快就看出了我的状况，他们让我做音乐测试，看我怎么通过，来自娱自乐。考试的内容是，当这些曲子演奏得更快或更慢时，我还能认出多少首曲子。当他们以那些方式演奏《天佑吾王》时，对我而言是非常费解的谜题。还有一个人的耳朵几乎和我的一样坏，说来奇怪，他竟然还会吹一点笛子。可有一次，我在音乐测试中赢了他。

但在剑桥，没有一项工作能像收集甲虫那样让我热忱，带给我如此多的乐趣。我纯粹是出于收集的热情，因为我没有解剖过它们，也很少把它们的外在特征与出版物中的描述相比较，但还是给它们命名了。有一天，我撕下老树皮，发现两只罕见的甲虫，便一手抓了一只；

然后我又看到了第三种，也是新的一种，我舍不得丢掉，于是我把右手拿着的那一种塞进嘴里。哎呀！它那时喷射出一种强烈的辛辣液体，灼烧了我的舌头，我不得不把那只甲虫吐出来，那只甲虫跟第三只甲虫一样不见了。

我在收集昆虫方面小有成就，并且发明了两种新方法；冬天，我雇了一个工人，把老树上的苔藓刮下来，装在一个大袋子里，又在从沼泽地运来的芦苇的驳船底部收集废弃物，这样我就得到了一些非常稀有的物种。正如诗人为发表自己的第一首诗而感到无比高兴一样，我在斯蒂芬斯的《英国昆虫图志》[1]中看到"由 C.达尔文先生记录"这些神奇的文字，更是咒语般使我心花怒放。把我引入昆虫学的是我的远房亲戚 W.达尔文·福克斯[2]，他当时在剑桥大学基督学院，是个聪明而又讨人喜欢的人，我和他关系很亲。后来我和剑桥三一学院的阿尔伯特·韦[3]很熟，一起出去收集。多年以后，韦成了一位著名的考古

---

[1] 詹姆斯·弗朗西斯·斯蒂芬斯（1792—1852），英国昆虫学家和博物学家。他以 12 卷的《英国昆虫学插图》（*Illustrations of British entomology*）闻名。

[2] 威廉·达尔文·福克斯（1805—1880），英国牧师、博物学家。

[3] 阿尔伯特·韦（1805—1874），英国古董商，也是英国皇家考古研究所的主要创始人，在剑桥期间他曾画过一幅达尔文手持虫网，骑在大甲虫上的漫画。

学家。我还与同一学院的 **H.** 汤普森[①]合作，他后来成了一位著名的农学家、一条大铁路的主席，以及英国的议员。从这时可见，收集甲虫的爱好似乎预示着前途的光明！

我很惊讶，我在剑桥看到的许多甲虫给我留下了难以磨灭的印象。我还能准确地记得我拍摄过的一些柱子、古树和河岸的样子。漂亮的十字偏须步甲（*Panagaeus cruxmajor*）[②]是我那时珍藏的宝贝，我在唐恩村[③]散步看到另一种甲虫跑过，立刻觉察到它和十字偏须步甲略有不同，这是郭公虫科 *Pelonides* 属 "四点"种（*P. quadripunctata*）[④]，这两个物种紧密联系，轮廓上有轻微不同。在那些日子里，我从来没有见过活着的畸颚步甲属物种[⑤]，在没有受过这类教育的人看来它和许多

① 哈里·梅赛－汤普森，第一代准男爵（1809—1874），致力于约克郡发展的农学研究者、铁路管理人及区议员，英国皇家农业协会创始人之一，英国东北铁路董事会主席。

② *Panagaeus cruxmajor*，昆虫纲鞘翅目步甲科偏须步甲属，红色背甲上有黑色十字，1758 年由林奈命名，中文为暂定译名。

③ 唐恩村，达尔文从成家立业至去世生活了四十多年的地方，伦敦外围的郊区。

④ *Pelonides quadripunctata*，昆虫纲鞘翅目郭公虫科甲虫，红色背甲上有呈田字排列的四个黑色点，1823 年由美国昆虫学家、海螺学家和爬虫学家托马斯·塞（1787—1834）命名，中文为推测名。

⑤ *Licinus*，昆虫纲鞘翅目步甲科畸颚步甲属，1802 年由 "现代昆虫学之父"、法国动物学家和天主教牧师皮埃尔·安德烈·拉特雷耶（1762—1833）命名。

其他黑色的肉食亚目步甲科物种几乎没有什么区别；前段时间我的儿子们在这里（英国）发现了一个标本，我能立刻意识到我从没见过。但毕竟我已经有二十年没仔细看过英国甲虫了。

到目前为止，我还没有提到过对我整个职业生涯影响最大的一件事——我和亨斯洛教授的友谊。在来剑桥之前，我从我哥哥那里听说过他，说他精通科学的每一个分支，因此我打算对他毕恭毕敬。他每周举行一次招待会，那时所有的本科生和大学的一些与科学有关的年长成员常常在晚上聚会。我很快通过福克斯受到了邀请，并经常去那里。不久，我就和亨斯洛熟了。我在剑桥的后半段时间，大都和他一起散步。因此，我被一些老师称为"与亨斯洛同行的人"，晚上，我经常被邀请参加他的家庭晚宴。他在植物学、昆虫学、化学、矿物学和地质学方面学识渊博。他最喜欢从长期的细致观察中得出结论。他的判断力极好，从不偏激；但我不认为有人会说他有什么独特的天赋。他笃信宗教，非常正统，以至于有一天他告诉我，如果三十九条信纲中的任何一个字被修改，他都会感到悲伤。他的道德品质在各方面都令人钦佩。他完全不虚荣，心胸宽大。我从来没有见过一个人如此不考虑自己和自己的利益。他脾气好得不能再好了，彬彬有礼，讨人喜欢。然而，正如我所看到的，任何不良行为都可能激起他的强烈愤慨和迅速反应。

我曾在剑桥的街道上看到几乎和法国大革命时期一样可怕的情景。有两个盗尸者被捕了，他们被押进监狱的时候，一群街头暴民把他们从警察手里扯了过来，拽着他们的腿拖过泥泞的石头路。他们从头到脚都是泥，脸上出的血不是被人踢的就是被石头砸的；他们看起来像死尸，但是人群太拥挤了，我只能瞥见几眼这些可怜的家伙。我活那么大，第一次见亨斯洛那样，面对这可怕的场景，脸上写满了愤怒，他多次试图穿过人群，但这根本不可能。然后他奔向市长，叫我别跟着他，要多找些警察来。我忘了当时是怎么发生这事的，只记得那俩人被关进监狱，逃过了一劫。

亨斯洛的善心是无限的，他为贫穷的教区居民制定了许多绝妙的计划证明了这一点。几年后，他在希契姆地区①工作、生活。我和这样一个人的亲密关系应该是一种不可估量的好处。我不得不提到一件小事，以表

---

① 英格兰萨福克郡的一个村庄和公民教区。

约翰·亨斯洛的画像，取自1913年《英国植物学的缔造者》（*Makers of British Botany*），由英国画家托马斯·赫伯特·马圭尔绘制。图片版权已进入公有领域

示他的善意。当我在潮湿的地面上检查花粉粒时，我看到了外露的花粉管，就立刻跑过去把我的惊奇发现告诉他。现在，我想任何其他的植物学教授看到我如此匆忙地赶来进行这样的交流，也忍不住会笑话我。但他赞许并说这种现象是多么有趣，并解释了为什么会这样，还让我清楚地明白，人们是如何发现它的；因此，我离开他时，一点也不感到羞愧，反而为自己发现了这么了不

起的事实而感到高兴，但我决定再也不那么匆忙地去分享我的发现。

惠威尔博士[①]是我认识的德高望重的人之一，他有时会来拜访亨斯洛，有几次我晚上和他一起走回家。在我聆听过的人当中，除了詹姆斯·麦金托什爵士之外，他是最善于谈论严肃话题的人。伦纳德·詹宁斯[②]（伦纳德·詹宁斯先生父亲的表兄是著名的索姆·詹宁斯[③]）后在博物学方面发表了几篇很好的文章，在我的《"小猎犬"号航行的动物学》[④]里写了鱼类的那一部分；他写了一长串论文，主要是动物学的，他经常和亨斯洛待在一起，亨斯洛是他的姐夫。我去他位于（斯瓦汉姆－布

---

① 威廉·惠威尔（1794—1866），博学的科学家、哲学家、基督教神学家。同时专精于数学与诗，他是最早从事科学史研究的史学家之一，创造了 scientist（科学家）和 physicist（物理学家）这两个词。
② 伦纳德·詹宁斯（1800—1893），后改姓布洛梅菲尔德，是一位英国牧师、作家和博物学家。他主要因其对一年中的详细物候观察而出名。著有《博物学的观察：该科学研究观察习惯的导论》（*Observations In Natural History：With An Introduction On Habits Of Observing*，1846）。
③ 索姆·詹宁斯（1704—1787），英国作家和国会议员。他是动物伦理的早期倡导者。
④ 所提到的书为查尔斯·达尔文编纂，5 位专门学者主笔的《菲茨罗伊船长指挥的英国军舰"小猎犬"号航行的动物学：1832—1836 年》，（*The Zoology of the Voyage of H.M.S. Beagle Under the Command of Captain Fitzroy，R.N.，during the Years 1832 to 1836*）。此书共分 5 部分，1838 年2 月至 1843 年 10 月期间陆续问世。

贝克）① 沼土区边界的牧师住宅区拜访过他，我们一起散步，谈论博物学。我还认识了几个比我年长的人，他们对科学不太感兴趣，但却是亨斯洛的朋友。一个是苏格兰人，亚历山大·拉姆齐爵士② 的兄弟，耶稣学院的教师。他是个讨人喜欢的人，但没活太久。另一位是道斯③ 先生，他后来是赫里福德的院长，以给贫困者施教的成功而闻名。这些人，还有其他地位相同的人，还有亨斯洛，有时会去乡下远游，我也被允许加入，他们非常乐意。

回想起来，我想我身上一定是有某种优于一般年轻人的点，否则上面提到的那些比我年长得多、学术地位高得多的人，就不会让我和他们交往。当然，我当时没有这种优越感，我记得我的一位运动爱好者的朋友特纳，他看到我研究甲虫，说我有一天会成为皇家学会④

①　斯瓦汉姆－布贝克（Swaffham Bulbeck）是英格兰东剑桥郡的一个小村庄。
②　亚历山大·拉姆齐爵士，第三代准男爵（1813—1875），英国保守党政治家。
③　理查德·道斯（1793年受洗，1867年逝世），英国神职人员和教育家。他从1850年起担任赫里福德学院院长。道斯在基础教育应用科学领域具有开创性贡献：他用启发式学习代替传统教学，并建立了一个初级实验室以促进简单科学实验。
④　"伦敦皇家自然知识促进学会"（Royal Society of London for Improving Natural Knowledge）的简称，该学会成立于17世纪，达尔文与1839年1月当选皇家学会会员。

的会员，当时在我看来，这个想法很荒谬。

在剑桥大学的最后一年，我认真而又饶有兴趣地阅读了洪堡[①]的《个人故事》。这一著作，以及赫歇尔爵士[②]的《自然哲学研究导论》激起了我强烈的热情，我想为博物学的崇高架构做出哪怕是最微不足道的贡献。没有哪本书对我的影响比这两本书更大。我大段大段地摘抄洪堡描写特内里费岛[③]的段落，并在我上述提及的一次远足中大声朗读，（我想我是）读给了亨斯洛、拉姆齐和道斯，因为前一次我已经谈到特内里费岛的光芒四射[④]，然后队伍中的一些人宣布他们会争取去那里；但我认为他们只是半认真的。不过，我是很认真的，有人给我介绍了一个伦敦商人，让我打听船只的情况。但这个计划当然是被我的"小猎犬"号航行打破了。

---

① 弗里德里希·亚历山大·冯·洪堡（1769—1859），德国地理学家、博物学家。他是普鲁士大臣、哲学家和语言学家威廉·冯·洪堡的弟弟。他对植物地理学的定量研究奠定了生物地理学领域的基础。著有《美洲赤道地区旅行的个人故事：1799—1804 年》（*Personal narrative of travels to the equinoctial regions of America, during the years 1799–1804*）。

② 约翰·赫歇尔爵士（1792—1871），活跃于数学、天文学、化学领域的英国博学家，发明家，并从事植物学工作。著有《自然哲学研究导论》（*Preliminary Discourse on the Study of Natural Philosophy*）。

③ 西班牙特内里费岛，是非洲海岸的那利群岛中最大岛屿，公认因火山作用形成，西班牙最高峰便位于该岛。

④ 此处较有可能是说明亚热带小岛的温暖多晴与英国的阴冷形成对比。

我的暑假被收集甲虫、阅读和短途旅行占据。到了秋天，我又把全部时间都花在了打猎上，主要是在伍德豪斯和美尔，有时和伊顿庄园的伊顿少爷[①]在一起。总的来说，在剑桥度过的三年是我幸福生活中最快乐的时光。因为那时我身体很好，几乎总是兴致勃勃。

我第一次来剑桥是在1828年的圣诞节，因而在我通过最终学校考试后，在1831年伊始，我被强制留校了两学期[②]。然后亨斯洛说服我开始研究地质学。因此，在我回到什罗普郡的时候，我检查了各个地区，并在地图上什鲁斯伯里周围地区做了标记。塞奇威克教授打算在八月初去北威尔士，在古老的岩石中进行他著名的地质调查，亨斯洛请求他带上我。[与这次行程有关的是我父亲告诉过我一个关于塞奇威克的故事：一天早晨，他们从酒店出发，走了两英里，塞奇威克突然停了下来，大声说要回去，因为确信"这该死的恶棍"（服务员）没有把自己托付给服务员的六便士给清理房间的女服务员。

---

① 托马斯·伊顿（1809—1880），英国博物学家，出生于惠灵顿以北威尔德荒原的西南边缘的伊顿庄园，此地位于英格兰什罗普郡的一个村庄和公民教区，他是查尔斯·达尔文的朋友和笔友。伊顿于1855年继承了庄园。
② 英国中小学及大学，一学年分为三个学期，秋季、冬季和春季，由于查尔斯·达尔文错过1828年的春季学期，不能按时毕业，因此大致是学校安排修够冬季和春季学期以完成学业，后文提到跟随亨斯洛和塞奇威克继续进修也证明了这一点。达尔文是在1831年6月份毕业于剑桥的。

他最终被成功劝阻，没有理由怀疑那个服务员突然不忠。——弗朗西斯·达尔文注］于是他来到我父亲家里过了夜。

那天晚上与塞奇威克的短暂交谈在我的脑海中留下了深刻的印象。在检查什鲁斯伯里附近的一个旧砾石坑时，一个工人告诉我，他在里面发现了一个很大的、磨损的热带螺壳，就像人们可以在乡村小屋的壁炉架上看到的那样；因为他不肯卖，我就相信他真的是在坑里找到的。我把这件事告诉了塞奇威克，他立刻（以坚定的语气）说，一定是有人把它扔进了坑里；但又补充道，如果它真的是埋在那里的，那将是地质学研究现状最大的不幸，因为它将推翻我们所有关于米德兰各郡浅层沉积物的知识。这些沉积的砾石层实际上是冰河时期的产物，而我若干年后在砾石层中发现了破碎的北极贝壳。但我当时还是完全惊讶于塞奇威克的反应竟不是高兴，在英国中部海面附近发现一个热带贝壳，该是个美妙的事啊。虽然我读过各种各样的科学书籍，但以前从来没有什么使我彻底认识到，科学就是把事实组合起来，以便从中得出一般规律或结论。

第二天早晨，我们动身去兰戈伦、康威、班戈和卡佩尔居里格^①。这次旅行对我了解一个国家的地质情况有一定的帮助。塞奇威克经常让我走一条与他平行的路线，让我把岩石标本带回来，并在地图上标出地质层。我毫不怀疑他这样做是为了我好，我这方面的知识太欠缺了，没能帮到他。在这次旅行中，我发现了一个令我震惊的实例：人们在观察到某种现象之前，不管这些现象是多么明显，都能轻易忽视。我们在伊德瓦尔峡谷^②待了好几个小时，极其小心地研究了所有的岩石，但因为塞奇威克急于在其中找到化石，我们谁也没有看见环绕我们的是多么奇妙的冰川现象。我们没有注意到那些刻痕分明的岩石，那些高处的大圆石，那些冰川的侧碛和终碛^③。然而，这些现象是如此明显，以致我在许多年后发表在《哲学杂志》^④（1842）上的一篇论文中指出，

① 这 4 个区域均位于英国北威尔士。

② 伊德瓦尔峡谷是北威尔士山区的国家公园，海拔较高，地势峻峭，吸引了登山者、攀岩者、地质学家和博物学家。

③ 冰碛指在冰川堆积作用过程中挟带和搬运的碎屑构成的堆积物，又称冰川沉积物。分布在冰川边缘的叫侧碛，随着冰川向前推进在冰川末端围绕冰舌的前端的冰碛物，叫终碛。

④ 《哲学杂志》是现存最古老的英文科学期刊之一。由亚历山大·蒂洛克于 1798 年创立，1822 年理查德·泰勒成为联合主编，由泰勒和弗朗西斯出版公司连续出版。达尔文发表文章时，该期刊名为"伦敦，爱丁堡和都柏林哲学杂志"（*The London，Edinburgh and Dublin Philosophical Magazine*），达尔文在该杂志上发表了多篇研究文章。

这座山谷清晰地讲述着自己故事，比一座被火烧毁的房子还清晰。如果它仍然被冰川填满，冰川作用的现象都没实际这么明显。

在卡佩尔居里格，我和塞奇威克分道扬镳，我用指南针和地图以直线距离穿过群山来到巴茅斯，不按任何路线走，除非说是路线与我重合。就这样，我来到了一些奇怪的荒野，非常喜欢这种旅行方式。我去巴茅斯看望了几位在那里读书的剑桥朋友，然后回到什鲁斯伯里，再到美尔庄园打猎。因为在那个时候，我要是为了地质学或其他科学而耽误了打鹧鸪①活动的头几天，我准会认为自己疯了。

---

① 又称"英国鹧鸪""灰山鹑"。

第 3 章

"小猎犬"号的航行

在北威尔士短暂的地质之旅结束后，我回到家中，发现亨斯洛给我寄了一封信，信里说，菲茨罗伊船长 [1] 愿意把船舱的一部分让给任何愿意作为博物学家与他一起参加"小猎犬"号航行 [2] 的年轻人。我相信，我已经在我的手稿日志中叙述了当时发生的所有

---

[1] 罗伯特·菲茨罗伊中将（1805—1865）是英国皇家海军军官和气象学家。他于 1828 年被任命为"小猎犬"号的船长。他对天气预报方法及气象局的建立做出突出贡献。任职新西兰总督期间，还试图保护毛利人免受英国定居者声索的非法土地销售。由于"菲茨罗伊"（FitzRoy）这个姓氏有"国王之子"之意，英国诺曼王朝贵族较早使用，因而成了后文所探讨的一个话题。

[2] 达尔文参与的这次环球航行为英国皇家海军"小猎犬"号（又称"比格尔"号、"贝格尔"舰）的第二次航行，此船因第一次经过南美洲比格尔海峡而得名。主要从英国普利茅斯港出发，经过亚速尔群岛、佛得角等大西洋岛屿，从南美西海岸部分沿海城市停靠并绕过德雷克海峡到达南美东海岸，经过新西兰、澳大利亚及太平洋诸岛，再越过非洲开普敦，最后经停南美再折返英国。原本计划两年内完成航行，实际上花了 5 年，达尔文为这段航行编写手稿日志，出版后获得了一定赞誉。

情况 ①；我在这里只想说，我当时急于接受这个提议，但我父亲强烈反对，并补充说"如果你能找到任何有常识的人建议你去，我会同意的"——这句话成了我的救命稻草。那天晚上我写信拒绝这个提议。第二天早上，我去美尔庄园为 9 月 1 日做准备，在打猎的时候，我的舅舅（约西亚·韦奇伍德二世）叫上我，提出开车送我去什鲁斯伯里和我父亲谈谈，因为我舅舅认为我接受这个邀约是明智的。我父亲一直认为我舅舅是世界上明智的人之一，他立刻以最友善的方式表示同意。因为之前我在剑桥时花钱相当大手大脚，为了安慰父亲，我说："我一定会在'小猎犬'号上小心花钱，把钱花在刀刃上！"他却笑着回答："但是他们都告诉我你很狡猾。"

第二天，我动身去剑桥会见亨斯洛，然后又去伦敦会见了菲茨罗伊，很快就把一切协商好了。后来我和菲茨罗伊能进行私下交谈了，我听说因为我鼻子的形状，

---

① 查尔斯·达尔文的"小猎犬"号航行手稿日志将会贯穿本部分至本书第 7 部分，1839 年 5 月首次出版为"手稿和评论"，为菲茨罗伊舰长编纂的《"小猎犬"号航行的记述》的第 3 部分。而 1845 年出版的修订后的第二版名为《环球航行期间访问的国家的博物和地质研究日志》。而后该书 1905 年再版更名为《"小猎犬"号航海记》，这个书名也成了该手稿出版的最常见的标题。

我险些被拒！菲茨罗伊是拉瓦特[1]的忠实信徒，深信自己可以根据一个人的面容轮廓来判断那人的品性；他曾质疑我这样鼻子的人是否对远航拥有足够的精力和坚定的决心。但我想他后来一定很满意我鼻子传达的是假象。

菲茨罗伊的性格非常独特，有许多高尚的特征：他忠于自己的职责，对他人的过失宽宏大量，勇敢、坚定、不屈不挠、精力充沛，是他所有船客的忠实朋友。他会不辞辛劳地帮助那些他认为值得帮助的人。他是一个英俊的男人，非常像一位绅士，举止非常有礼貌。在里约时，使节告诉我，菲茨罗伊的舅舅是著名的卡斯尔雷勋爵[2]。尽管如此，他一定是从查理二世[3]那里继承了

---

[1]　约翰·卡斯帕·拉瓦特（1741—1801），瑞士诗人、作家、哲学家、相术师和神学家。

[2]　罗伯特·斯图亚特，卡斯尔雷子爵（1769—1822），是一位盎格鲁－爱尔兰政治家和外交家。他因致力于镇压1798年爱尔兰地区的叛乱并确保1800年《爱尔兰联合法案》的通过而发迹于政坛。从1812年起担任英国外交大臣，他是击败拿破仑的联盟的核心，并在维也纳会议上担任英国全权代表。在利物浦勋爵的战后政府中，他被视为反对改革。1822年，他在任职期间自杀。

[3]　斯图亚特王朝的国王查理二世（1630—1685），斯图亚特王朝（1371—1714）是由法国布列塔尼半岛的斯图亚特家族在英国实行君主统治而得名，该时代由于资产阶级力量的壮大，爆发了处决君主、短暂共和、王权复辟、光荣革命等一系列与资产阶级革命有关的历史事件。

很多外貌特征，因为沃利奇博士 ① 给了我一组他拍的照片，我惊奇地发现有一张和菲茨罗伊很相似；一看这个名字，我就发现是阿尔巴尼伯爵——索别斯基·斯图亚特 ②，同一位君主的后裔。

菲茨罗伊的暴脾气是最令人不快的，在清晨通常最为糟糕。他如鹰一般犀利的眼光总能察觉到船上有什么不对劲，然后毫不留情地指责。他对我很好，但难以产生亲密的关系，因为他不是那种和我很处得来的人，我们会因一些问题吵起来。我们吵过好几次；例如，在航程早期，在巴西北部的巴伊亚航行的时候，他捍卫并赞扬了我所憎恶的奴隶制，并告诉我，他刚刚拜访了一位大奴隶主，他传唤了自己的许多奴隶，问他们是否不够幸福，他们是否希望自由，所有人都回答"不"。然后我近乎讥讽地反诘：难道奴隶们在主人面前的回答也算

① 乔治·沃利奇（1815—1899），英国医生、海洋生物学家和专业摄影师。父亲丹麦博物学家纳撒尼尔·沃利奇是皇家植物园的负责人。1860年，他陪同利奥波德·麦克林托克爵士乘坐"小猎犬"号横渡北大西洋，为铺设拟议的跨大西洋电缆勘测海底。他在1898年获得了林奈奖章，以表彰他在探索深海动物群方面所做的宝贵工作。
② 约翰·索别斯基·斯图亚特和查尔斯·爱德华·斯图亚特，为19世纪20年代两个英国兄弟约翰·卡特·艾伦（1795—1872）和查尔斯·曼宁·艾伦（1802—1880）采用的名字。大约在1839年开始声称他们的父亲托马斯·艾伦（1767—1852），前皇家海军中尉，是詹姆斯二世之子查尔斯·爱德华·斯图亚特的唯一子女。但其真实性一直存有争议。

站得住脚的论据？这让他非常生气，他说，因为我怀疑他的话，我们不能再一起生活了。我本以为我会该被迫离开这艘船；消息很快就传开了，但当船长为平息自己的愤怒而派舰务官来羞辱我，我收到下级军官舱全体军官的邀请，希望我能跟他们一起，这让我如释重负。但几小时后，菲茨罗伊表现出了他一贯的宽宏大量，他派了一名警官来向我道歉，并要求我继续与他住在一起。

他的性格在几个方面是我所见过最高尚的。

"小猎犬"号的航行是迄今为止我生命中最重要的事件，并决定了我的整个职业生涯；然而，这取决于一个小机缘，我舅舅愿意开车三十英里送我去什鲁斯伯里（没几个舅舅可以做得到），还有我鼻子的形状这样的小事。我一直觉得，由于这次航行，我的头脑得到了第一次真正的训练或教育；我被引导密切关注博物学的几个分支，因此我的观察能力得到了提高，尽管它们一直是相当发达的。

对所有参观过的地方进行的地质调查至关重要，因为推理发挥了作用。在首次考察一个新的区域时，没有比岩石的混乱更令人绝望的了；但是，通过记录岩石和化石在许多地方的分层和性质，不断地推理和预测其

达尔文（右四）在"小猎犬"号上的画像（身穿燕尾服背对画面），特聘画家奥古斯塔斯·厄尔于1832年在阿根廷海港附近所作的漫画，右六背影可能是菲茨罗伊船长。图片版权已进入公有领域

他地方会发现什么，对该地区的研究很快就开始迎来曙光，整体结构或多或少变得清晰。我当时带了莱尔的《地质学原理》①的第一卷，我认真学习了这本书；这书在很多方面对我都有极大的帮助。我考察的第一个地方，即佛得角群岛的圣加戈，就清楚地证明了莱尔在地质学的研究方式，与我身边或后来读过的任何其他人的

① 《地质学原理：通过参考现在运行的原因来解释地球表面以前的变化》（*Principles of Geology: Being an Attempt to Explain the Former Changes of the Earth's Surface, by Reference to Causes Now in Operation*）是苏格兰地质学家查尔斯·莱尔（1797—1875）的作品，于1830年至1833年出版了3卷。莱尔，又译"赖尔""莱伊尔"，曾任伦敦地质学会会长，下文中莱尔及其作品将多次出现。

作品相比，具有惊人的优越性。

我的另一项职业是收集各类动物，简要描述并大致解剖许多海洋动物；但是，由于我不能画画，没有足够的解剖学知识，我在航行中制作的一大堆"手稿"几乎毫无用处。可以说我浪费了很多时间，但那些花在获取甲壳亚门类动物知识上的时间并没有浪费，因为多年后，当我写蔓足下纲的专著时，这还是很有用的。

在一天的某个时候，我写日志，耐着性子地把我所看到的一切仔细生动地描述出来；这是一个很好的实践。我的日志也有一部分是写给我家的信，一有机会就寄到英国。

然而，上述各种专题研究的重要性，比不上我所获得的十足干劲，以及我对自己所从事的一切的那种专注与兴致勃勃。我所想或所读的一切都与我所看到或可能看到的东西直接相关；在航行的五年里，这种思维习惯一直延续着。我确信正是这种训练支持了我在科学领域所做的一切。

回顾过去，我现在可以感觉到，我对科学的热爱逐渐超越了其他爱好。在最初的两年里，我对打猎还有满腔热情，我还会去打一些鸟类和小动物来收藏；但渐渐地，我越来越多地把枪交给了我的雇工①，最后完全交给了他，因为打猎干扰了我的工作，尤其是对了解一个国家的地质结构。我发现观察和推理的乐趣潜移默化地改变了我，远超于技巧和运动带来的乐趣。我父亲是我见过的最敏锐的观察者，他有一种怀疑的性格，而且一点也不相信颅相学，因为在航行后第一次见到我时，他对我通过旅行中的探求导致思维的成长表示肯定，他转过身来对我的姐妹们喊道："哎呀，他的头型完全变了。"

下面继续谈论我的航行经过。1831 年 9 月 11 日，我和菲茨罗伊到去普利茅斯港看了一次"小猎犬"号。从那里我回到什鲁斯伯里，与我的父亲和姐妹们做一次长时间的道别。10 月 24 日起我在普利茅斯暂居，一直待到 12 月 27 日，"小猎犬"号终于离开英格兰海岸环游世界。

西姆斯·科文顿，达尔文在"小猎犬"号上的雇员。图片版权已进入公有领域

① 指的是西姆斯·科文顿（1816—1861），"小猎犬"号上的客船服务员，也是位小提琴手，1833—1839 年受雇于查尔斯·达尔文，协助其进行航行考察。

我们曾两次尝试航行，但每次都被大风吹回。在普利茅斯的这两个月是我所度过的最痛苦的时光，尽管我使出各种办法，但无济于事。一想到要离开我所有的家人和朋友这么长时间，我就心烦意乱，天气似乎阴沉得无法形容。我也有心悸和心脏疼痛的困扰，像许多无知的年轻人一样，尤其是一个只有一点点医学知识的人，我确信自己患有心脏病。我没有咨询任何医生，因为我完全相信他们的答复是我不适合这次航行，因此我决心不惜冒一切危险出发。

我在这里不需要提及我们所去的航程中发生的很多事件以及我们所做的事情，因为我已经在我出版的"日志"上给出了充分的描述。现在热带植被的壮丽比其他任何东西都更加生动地呈现在我的脑海中；南美巴塔哥尼亚的大沙漠和火地岛森林覆盖的群山激发了我对宏伟壮丽的认知，给我留下了不可磨灭的印象。看到一个赤身裸体、充满野性的当地人是一件我永远不会忘记的事情。我骑马穿越荒野国家或乘船旅行的许多经历都非常有趣，其中一些旅行持续了好几个星期：旅行中的不适和某种程度的危险在当时根本不算什么，后来也没有再发生过。我还对自己的一些科学工作感到非常满意，例如解决珊瑚岛问题，以及确定某些岛屿的地质结构，例如圣赫勒拿岛。我也无法忽略自己在加拉帕戈斯群岛（科隆群岛）①的发现：几个岛屿上的动植物之间有着独特关系，以及所有这些动植物与南美洲居民之间也有着独特关系。

据我自己判断，我在航行中尽了最大的努力，完全出于调查的乐趣，也出于在自然科学的大量事实中尽自己一份力的强烈愿望。但我也雄心勃勃地想在科学界人士中占据一个明显位置，无论我的这股劲是多于还是少于大多数同行，我没有任何意见。

圣贾戈的地质情况令人惊叹，但也很简单：一股熔岩曾流过海床，之后堆积了碎的新贝壳和珊瑚，并被晒烤成为坚硬的白色岩石。那之后，整个岛屿都被抬升了。但白色岩石的线条向我揭示了一个新的重要事实，即火山口周围后来发生了沉降，此后火山口开始活动，并喷出了熔岩。然后我第一次意识到，我可能会写一本关于访问过的各个国家的地质学的书，这让我兴奋不已。那对我来说是一个难忘的时刻，我多么清楚地回

①　加拉帕戈斯群岛（西班牙语中意为"陆龟群岛"），1832 年，厄瓜多尔共和国从西班牙手中夺得加拉帕戈斯群岛的主权，将该群岛官方命名为科隆群岛。该群岛是东太平洋跨越赤道的火山群岛，离厄瓜多尔本土 1100 千米。

想起了自己在低矮的熔岩峭壁下休息，当时烈日炙烤，我附近生长着几株奇怪的沙漠植物，脚下的潮池里有活珊瑚。在航行的晚些时候，菲茨罗伊听我读了一些自己的日记，宣布它值得出版；所以当时第二本书指日可待！[①]

在航程接近尾声时，我在阿森松岛[②]收到了一封信，信中我的姐妹们告诉我，塞奇威克拜访了我的父亲，并说我应该在顶尖的科学家中占有一席之地。当时我不明白他怎么会了解我的进程，但我后来听说亨斯洛在剑桥哲学学会[③]面前读了我之前写给他的一些信（在1835年11月16日举行的会议上读过，并印在一本31页的小册子中，供该学会成员内部阅读）。我收集的化石被送到亨斯洛那里，引起了古生物学家的极大关注。读完这封信后，我蹦蹦跳跳爬上阿森松山，用地质锤敲击火山岩，聆听它们的回响。这一切都表明我是多么雄心勃勃！但我想我可以实话实说，多年后，尽管我最关心的

① 此处有可能是说达尔文参与的两部"小猎犬"号航行作品——《"小猎犬"号航行的动物学》和《"小猎犬"号航行的记述》。

② 阿森松岛位于大西洋海岭，在行政区划上属于圣赫勒拿岛，为英属殖民地，在达尔文时期是一个熔岩荒岛，后来达尔文、胡克等人进行了植被改造后已适宜居住。

③ 剑桥哲学学会（1819年至今）由爱德华·克拉克、亚当·塞奇威克和约翰·史蒂文斯·亨斯洛创立，是剑桥最古老的科学学会。

是莱尔和胡克①这样的人的认可，他们是我的朋友，但我并不太关心公众的言论。我并不是说，我没有因为我的书受到的好评或销量可观感到高兴，但这种快乐是短暂的，我相信我从不会为了追名逐利而偏离正轨。

---

① 约瑟夫·道尔顿·胡克爵士（1817—1911），英国植物学家和探险家，地理植物学的创始人，也是查尔斯·达尔文最亲密的朋友。后接替父亲威廉·杰克逊·胡克担任英国邱园皇家植物园园长，并获得了英国科学界的最高荣誉。

第4章

回到英国至走向婚姻

这两年零三个月是我最活跃的时光，虽然我偶尔不舒服，并荒废了一些时间。在什鲁斯伯里、美尔、剑桥和伦敦之间来回了好几次之后，12 月 13 日我在剑桥（菲兹威廉路）租房住下，我所有的藏品都由亨斯洛妥善保管。我在这里住了三个月，在米勒教授[①]的帮助下检查了我的矿物和岩石。

我开始准备我的"旅行日志"，这不是一项艰苦的工作，因为我的手稿札记写得很仔细，我的主要工作是对我更有趣的科学成果进行摘要。应莱尔的要求，我还向地质学会[②]发送了一份关于我观察到的智利海岸抬升的简

---

① 威廉·哈罗丝·米勒（1801—1880），威尔士矿物学家，奠定了现代晶体学的基础。"米勒指数"以他的名字命名。

② 本部分及之后提到的"地质学会"均为伦敦地质学会（1807 年至今），达尔文于 1837 年当选委员会成员，1838—1841 年任学会秘书，并在《地质学会会议记录》和《地质学会学报》上发表过多篇研究。

查尔斯·莱尔，摄影师梅奥尔。图片版权已进入公有领域

短报告[1]（地质学会会议记录，ii，1838，第446-449页）。

1837年3月7日，我到伦敦的大马尔伯勒街租住了近两年，直到结婚。在这两年里，我完成了我的日志，在地质学会读了几篇论文，开始为我的"地质观测"[2]

---

[1] 《对智利海岸近期海拔升高的观察证据，其于在菲茨罗伊船长统率下的皇家"小猎犬"号上的调查》（Observations of proofs of recent elevation on the coast of Chili, made during the survey of His Majesty's Ship Beagle commanded by Capt. FitzRoy R.N.），为达尔文在伦敦地质学会发表的第一篇文章。

[2] 此书为达尔文陆续出版了两本"地质观测"书，分别为1844年出版的《火山岛地质观测》（Geological Observations on the Volcanic Islands, visited during the Voyage of H.M.S. Beagle）和1846年出版的《南美洲地质观测》（Geological Observations on South America），为达尔文继《珊瑚礁》后的第二和第三部专著。

准备手稿，并为《"小猎犬"号航行的动物学》的出版作编排，同年 7 月，我开始了第一本笔记的写作，为我的《物种起源》准备素材，这个问题我已经思考了很长时间，并且在接下来的 20 年里笔耕不辍。

在这两年里，我还多少参与了一些学会的活动，并成为地质学会的名誉秘书之一。我见过莱尔很多次。他的一个主要特点是对别人工作的赞同。我回到英国后，向他解释我对珊瑚礁的看法时，他表现出的兴趣使我又惊又喜。他的建议和示范对我产生了很大的影响，这使我深受鼓舞。在这段时间里，我见了好几次罗伯特·布朗[1]；我过去常常在他周日早餐时间拜访，他滔滔不绝地说了许多稀奇的发现和有洞察力的评论，但它们几乎总是细枝末节，他从来没有和我讨论过科学中的问题。

这两年里，我进行了几次短途旅行放松，还有一次

---

[1]　罗伯特·布朗（1773—1858），苏格兰植物学家和古植物学家。他的贡献包括对细胞核和细胞质流的最早详细描述；"布朗运动"这一概念的创始人；第一个认识到裸子植物和被子植物之间的根本区别；他还为植物分类学做出了许多贡献，给定的许多植物拉丁学名至今仍在使用。

去了格伦罗伊平行道①，并写了一篇文章。这篇文章发表在《哲学学报》②上（1839年，第39—82页）。然而，这篇论文非常失败，我为此感到羞愧。我对南美洲陆地的海拔高度印象深刻，我把平行道的形成归因于海洋的作用；但当阿加西③提出他的冰川湖理论时，我不得不放弃我的观点。因为在我们当时的知识状态下，没有其他解释是可能的；我的错误给了我一个很好的教训，让我永远不要把排他作为一种科学信仰。

由于我不能整天从事科学工作，这两年我读了各种主题的书，包括形而上学、玄学派的书；但我并不适合这样的研究。大约在这个时候，我非常喜欢华兹华斯④和柯勒

① 格伦罗伊（苏格兰盖尔语意为"红色峡谷"）位于苏格兰高地洛哈伯地区，是由三个平行湖道地阶的地质现象而闻名的峡谷。从远处看，它们就像沿着峡谷一侧的人造道路，因此得名。大部分峡谷被指定为国家级自然保护。这里独特的地质地貌吸引了查尔斯·莱尔、查尔斯·达尔文等众多地质研究者考察调研。

② 学报为《英国皇家学会哲学学报》，达尔文发表的论文名为"对格伦罗伊平行道和苏格兰洛哈伯其地区的观察，试图证明它们起源于海洋"（Observations on the parallel roads of Glen Roy，and other parts of Lochaber in Scotland，with an attempt to prove that they are of marine origin）。

③ 路易·阿加西（1807—1873），瑞士出生的美国生物学家和地质学家，地球自然史的学者，其1840年关于格伦罗伊是冰川湖作用的论文，可看作是对达尔文1839年关于海洋作用论文的否定。

④ 威廉·华兹华斯（1770—1850），英国浪漫主义诗人，他与塞缪尔·柯勒律治联合出版《抒情歌谣》（1798年）帮助开启了英国文学的浪漫主义时代。代表作有短诗《我似孤云独自游》、长诗《远足》。

律治①的诗歌；我可以自豪地说我读了两遍《远足》。以前，弥尔顿②的《失乐园》是我最喜欢的，在"小猎犬"号的航行中，当我只能拿一本书时，我总是选择弥尔顿的。

火地岛风景，康拉德·马滕斯（1801—1878）绘于"小猎犬"号。图片版权已进入公有领域

① 塞缪尔·泰勒·柯勒律治（1772—1834），英国诗人、文学评论家、哲学家、神学家，与朋友威廉·华兹华斯共同创立了英国浪漫主义运动。1798年曾获约西亚·韦奇伍德二世资助继续从事文学创作。代表作有长诗《古舟子咏》。

② 约翰·弥尔顿（1608—1674），英国诗人和知识分子，著有史诗《失乐园》。

第 5 章

在伦敦

（说完了他幸福的婚姻生活和他的孩子后，他接着说：……[1]）

我们居住在伦敦的三年零八个月里，我的科学工作减少了，尽管比我生命中其他同等时间内的要少，但我尽可能地努力工作着。这是由于我的身体经常反复出现不适，还有一种严重的慢性病[2]。这段时间我能做，且做得更有意义的事则是把大部分的时间用在了《珊瑚礁》[3]的撰写，这是我结婚前就着手做的事，其中最后一次图书校样是在 1842 年 5 月 6 日。这本书虽然很小，但

---

① 此处为弗朗西斯·达尔文对原手稿的删略。

② 查尔斯·达尔文的健康多次受到多种罕见症状的影响，使他在很长一段时间内都处于严重的虚弱状态。他的病因至今存在多种解释，其中有一种解释是受蚊虫叮咬，得上"南美锥虫病"。

③ 全书名为《珊瑚礁的结构和分布，菲茨罗伊上尉指挥，"小猎犬"号航行地质学的第一部分，1832—1836》（ *The Structure and Distribution of Coral Reefs* , *Being the first part of the geology of the voyage of the Beagle* , *under the command of Capt. Fitzroy* , *R.N. during the years 1832 to 1836* ），为达尔文的第一部专著。

却花费了我 20 个月的努力，因为我必须阅读每一部关于太平洋岛屿的作品，并查阅各类海图。它受到科学界人士的高度评价，我认为，书中的理论到现在已经很成熟了。

我的其他书都没有像这本如此基于推论，整个理论体系都是先通过构思出南美洲西海岸，再看到真正的珊瑚礁。因此，我只需通过仔细检查活礁来验证和扩展我的观点。但值得注意的是，在过去的两年里，我一直在不停地关注陆地的间歇性上升，以及沉积物对南美洲海岸的剥蚀和堆积作用。这自然而然地促使我对沉降作用进行了深入思考——我通过珊瑚礁的向上生长想象沉积物的持续堆积。这样便建立了我的堡礁和环礁理论。

除了我在珊瑚礁方面的作品，在伦敦居住期间，我在地质学会面前阅读了有关南美洲大漂砾的论文[1]（地质学会会议记录，iii，1842），关于地震[2]（地质学会学报，

---

[1]　文章名为"南美洲漂砾和同时期无层理沉淀物的分布"（On the distribution of the erratic boulders and on the contemporaneous unstratified deposits of South America）。

[2]　文章名为"南美洲某些火山现象的联系，以及山脉和火山的形成，抬升大陆的相同力量"（On the connexion of certain volcanic phenomena in South America；and on the formation of mountain chains and volcanos，as the effect of the same powers by which continents are elevated），文章的形成是受"小猎犬"号航行期间亲历 1835 年智利地震的影响。

v，1840），关于蚯蚓松土、沃土作用的形成 [1]（地质学会会议记录，ii，1838）。我还继续负责《"小猎犬"号航行的动物学》的出版工作，我也从未停止收集与物种起源有关的证据；就算我病到无法做其他事，我还是坚持收集。

1842 年夏天，我的身体又比之前强健了，还独自去北威尔士参观了一下，目的是观察古老的冰川在填满大山谷时的作用。我就所见所闻在《哲学杂志》上发表了一篇简短报告（哲学杂志，1842）[2]。这次远足让我非常愉快，这是我最后一次健壮地为地质工作去爬山或远足。

在伦敦生活的初期，我还有足够的精力经常接触学会，见到了许多科学人士，以及其他各类有声望的人。我会心怀敬意地给出一些我的印象，尽管我没有什么可说的。

在我结婚前后，我见到莱尔的次数比见任何人都多。在我看来，他的头脑清晰、谨慎，能做出正确的判

---

① 文章名为 "论松土、沃土作用的形成"（On the formation of mould）。
② 本书第 2 部分提到的论文，文章标题为 "关于卡那封郡古冰川的影响，以及浮冰对巨石的搬运作用"（Notes on the effects produced by the ancient glaciers of Caernarvonshire，and on the boulders transported by floating ice）。

达尔文与长子，摄于 1842 年，图片最早公开于数学家卡尔·皮尔逊于 1914 年编纂的《弗朗西斯·高尔顿自传》。图片来源：Heritage Images/ 视觉中国

断，很有独创性。在我对他发表地质学的论断时，他总会穷追不舍，直至看清整体，并且经常能让我看得比以前更清晰。他会对我的提议提出所有可能的异议，即使这话题已穷尽，他也会长期持怀疑态度。他的第二个特点便是他会对其他科学家的工作表示由衷赞许。（这里可以看到稍微有点重复，这是由于有关莱尔等人的笔记

在 1881 年 4 月，也就是其余的"回忆录"写出来后的几年里才添加进来）

我从"小猎犬"号航行归来后，向莱尔解释了我对珊瑚礁的看法，这与他看法完全不同。他表现出了浓厚的兴趣，让我感受到惊讶和鼓舞。他热衷于科学，对人类未来的进步有着由衷的兴趣。他心地善良，宗教信仰上十分开明，更贴切地说是抱有怀疑态度；但他又坚定地相信神的存在。他极为正直，表现便是他成了同族源遗传理论①的"皈依者"，尽管他因反对拉马克的观点而声名鹊起，但这是在他年老之后。他提起我和他多年前的一段往事，当时我俩在讨论老派地质学家反对他的新观点，我曾说："如果每个科研人在 60 岁时寿终正寝该多好，那样他们就不会全盘否定新学说了。"说到这，他表示还是希望自己能被允许继续活下去。

我坚信莱尔对地质学的贡献超出之前的所有人。当我开始"小猎犬"号的航行时，睿智的亨斯洛和所有其他地质学家一样，在那时相信灾变的连续性，他建议我

---

① 此处的英文为"Descent theory"，"Descent"一词意为"血统，家族"。由查尔斯·达尔文在 1859 年《物种起源》一书中发展成"族源"和"同源"理论，将生物的起源通过共同祖先建立起联系。达尔文在 1871 年也发表了《人类的由来和性选择》（*The Descent of Man*，*and Selection in Relation to Sex*），对族源理论进行了再发展。

把当时刚刚出版的《地质学原理》第一卷拿来研读，但决不接受其中倡导的观点。现在，人们谈论《地质学原理》的方式会大有不同！我很自豪地记得，我在佛得角群岛进行地质考察的第一个地方，即圣地亚哥岛[1]，使我确信莱尔的观点比我所知的任何其他作品中所倡导的观点都具有极大的优越性。

莱尔作品的强大影响以前可以从法国和英国科学的不同进展中清楚地看到。埃利·德·博蒙特[2]的狂野假设，如他的"凹坑抬升"和"抬升线"（后者在地质学会被塞奇威克夸到了天上），目前虽被完全遗忘，但可能很大程度上借鉴了莱尔的。

我看过很多罗伯特·布朗的作品，他被洪堡称为"植物学的出色领导者"[3]。在我看来，他的非凡之处主要在于他精准、细致入微的观察。他的知识非常渊博，很多没发表的直接带进了棺材，因为他过分害怕犯错误。他毫无保留地向我灌输自己的知识，但在某些方面却出

---

① 佛得角群岛最大的一个岛屿。

② 让-巴蒂斯特·埃利·德·博蒙特（1798—1874），法国地质学家，绘制过英国和法国的地质图，法国科学院成员，柏林科学院、爱丁堡皇家学会、伦敦皇家学会的外籍会员，他将山脉起源归因于地球缓慢冷却和收缩引起的灾难性剧变。

③ 此处原文用了拉丁语，其中"facile Princeps"（出色的领导者）语源系西方教会中形成的说法。

奇地提防。在"小猎犬"号出航前，我拜访了他两三次，有一次他让我用显微镜观察并描述我看到的东西。我做了，现在我相信这是某种植物细胞质的奇妙流动。然后我问他我看到的是什么，但他回答我："这是我的小秘密。"

他非常友善。当他老了，身体很不健康，非常不适合做任何运动时，（正如胡克告诉我的那样）每天还去拜访一位住的离自己很远的老仆人（他资助着老仆人），并大声地为老人朗读图书。他的友善足以弥补他在科学上的任何吝啬和提防了。

我想在这里提到其他几位名人，我偶尔也见过他们，但关于他们，我没有什么值得一提的。我对 J. 赫歇尔爵士深表敬意，很高兴和他一起在好望角他那迷人的房子里吃饭，后来又在他伦敦的家里吃饭。我还见过他几次。他从不多说话，但他说的每一句话都值得一听。

我有一次在 R. 默奇森爵士①的家里吃早餐时遇到了著名的洪堡，这使我倍感荣幸，因为他表达了想要见我的意愿。预期可能太高了，因此对这位伟人有点失望。关于我们的面谈，我记不得太多，只记得洪堡非常高

---

① 罗德里克·因佩·默奇森爵士，第一代准男爵（1792—1871），英国地质学家，因调查和描述志留纪、泥盆纪和二叠纪系统而闻名。

兴，说了很多话。

××① 让我想起了我在亨斯利·韦奇伍德家遇到巴克尔②。我非常高兴，从他那里学到了收集证据的方法。他告诉我，他买下了所有他读过的书，并对每一本书都做了一个完整的索引，列出了他认为可能对他有用的事实依据，而且他总能记住在每书上读过的任何东西，因为他的记忆力很好。我问他如何判断哪些证据是有用的，他回答说他不知道，但一种直觉指引着他。由于这种编制索引的习惯，他得以在各种主题上给出数量惊人的参考文献，这可以在他的《文明史》中找到印证。我觉得这本书特别有趣，读了两遍，但我怀疑他的概括是否有价值。巴克尔是一个非常健谈的人，我几乎一直在听他说话，我也确实不能打断，因为他没有留下任何打断的机会。法勒太太③ 开始唱歌时，我跳起来说我必须听她唱歌；我走后，他转过身对一位朋友说（我哥哥无意中听到的）："好吧，读达尔文先生的书比与他谈话好

① 此处为弗朗西斯·达尔文对原手稿的删略。
② 亨利·托马斯·巴克尔（1821—1862），自学成才的英国历史学家，著有未完成的《英格兰文明史》，也是一位实力雄厚的业余国际象棋棋手。
③ 亨斯利·韦奇伍德家的二女儿，嫁给托马斯·亨利·法勒（1819—1899），第一代法勒男爵，英国公务员和统计学家。

多了。"

在其他伟大的文学家中，我曾在米尔曼教长[①]的家里遇到过西德尼·史密斯[②]。他说的每一句话都有一种无法言喻的趣味性，这也许在一定程度上是因为人们期待着被逗乐。他说到科克夫人时，当时她已经很老了。他继续讲道，这位女士在他的一次慈善布道上深受感动，从一位朋友那里借了一个几尼[③]放进盘子里。他评论道："人们普遍认为，我亲爱的老朋友科克夫人当时肯定鬼迷心窍了"。他这样说，以至于丝毫没有人怀疑他的意思是老太太被魔鬼施了咒，我不知道他是如何表达这一点的。

我也曾在斯坦霍普勋爵[④]（历史学家）的家里遇到过麦考利[⑤]，因为晚餐上除我之外只有一位客人，我有机会

---

① 亨利·哈特·米尔曼（1791—1868），英国历史学家和牧师，1849年当选英国圣保罗大教堂教长，是个诙谐幽默的人。
② 悉尼·史密斯（1771—1845）是一位英国作家和圣公会牧师。
③ 几尼是英格兰王国以及后来的英国在1663年至1813年所发行的铸币，面值很小。
④ 菲利普·亨利·斯坦霍普（1805—1875），第5代斯坦霍普伯爵，英国古物学家和保守党政治家。他在文化事业和历史著作撰写上都有较高建树，1816年至1855年间被封为马洪子爵。
⑤ 托马斯·宾顿·麦考利（1800—1859），第一代麦考利男爵，英国历史学家和辉格党政治家，在印度引入西式教育体系的主要人物。他的历史著作有《英格兰史》。

听到他谈话，他非常和蔼可亲。他话一点也不多；这样的人也确实也说不了太多，只要别人转变了话题，而他又允许话题的转移。

斯坦霍普勋爵曾经给我一个奇怪的小证据来证明麦考利记得准、记得全：许多历史学家过去经常在斯坦霍普勋爵的家里聚会，在讨论各种问题时，他们有时会与麦考利观点有所不同，以前他们经常查阅一些书来判断谁是对的；但最近，正如斯坦霍普勋爵所注意到的那样，那些历史学家都不再费这个劲了，麦考利所说的一切都是结论性的。

还有一次，我在斯坦霍普勋爵的家里遇到了他的一个由历史学家和其他文学人士组成的团体，其中包括莫特利[1]和格罗特[2]。午饭后，我和格罗特在车维宁公园散步将近一个小时。我对他的谈话很感兴趣，对他的举止简单而不做作感到高兴。

很久以前，我偶尔与历史学家菲利普·斯坦霍普的父亲共进晚餐。他是个奇怪的人。我对他所知甚少，

---

[1] 约翰·洛思罗普·莫特利（1814—1877），美国作家和外交官，亚伯拉罕·林肯政府的美国驻奥地利大使。著有三卷本《荷兰共和国的崛起》和四卷本《荷兰统一史》。

[2] 乔治·格罗特（1794—1871），英国古典历史学家，主要著作有《希腊历史》。

却很喜欢他。他坦率、亲切且令人愉快。他五官很有特点，面色棕黄，我见他的时候他全身衣服都是棕色的。他似乎相信一切别人认为完全不可思议的东西。有一天，他对我说："你为什么不放弃你那琐碎的地质学和动物学，转向神秘科学？"到场的历史学家，即马洪勋爵，似乎对他这么说话感到震惊，他迷人的妻子则被逗乐了。

我最后要提到的人是卡莱尔[1]，我在我哥哥家见过几次，在我自己家见过两三次。他讲话非常生动有趣，就像他的作品一样，但他有时在同一主题上讲得太长。我记得在哥哥家吃了一顿有趣的晚餐，除卡莱尔之外还有巴贝奇[2]和莱尔，他们都喜欢聊天。然而，卡莱尔却在整个晚宴上大肆宣扬沉默的好处，让大家都沉默了。晚饭后，巴贝奇以他最冷酷的态度感谢卡莱尔对沉默发表了非常有趣的讲话。

卡莱尔几乎对每一个人都嗤之以鼻。有一天，在我

---

[1] 托马斯·卡莱尔（1795—1881），苏格兰散文家、历史学家和哲学家，撰写过《法国大革命：一段历史》《历史上的英雄》《腓特烈大帝（普鲁士）》。

[2] 查尔斯·巴贝奇（1791—1871），英国博学家、数学家、哲学家、发明家和机械工程师，巴贝奇发明了第一台机械计算机——差分机，最终导致了更复杂的电子设计，他提出了数字可编程计算机的概念。被一些人认为是"计算机之父"。

家里，他把格罗特的"历史"称为"一个恶臭的泥潭，没有任何精神上的东西"。在他的《回忆录》问世前[①]，我一直认为他的冷笑部分是笑话，但现在似乎不是。他的表现是忧郁，几乎沮丧但又仁慈的；如果有一天他开怀大笑，那他的人设就要崩塌了。我相信他的仁慈是真实的，尽管更像是惴惴不安。在我看来，没有人能质疑他描绘事物和人物的非凡能力，这比麦考利的任何刻画都生动得多，但他刻画的人是否真实则是另一个问题。

卡莱尔可以把一些伟大的道德真理印在人的脑海里，这种能力简直无敌。但另一方面，他对奴隶制的看法令人反感。在他眼里，强权即公理。在我看来，他的思想非常狭隘；即便把他鄙视的所有科学分支都排除在外。令我惊讶的是，金斯利[②]竟然说他是一个非常适合推进科学发展的人。卡莱尔蔑视这样一种观点：一个数学家，比如惠威尔，可以判断歌德对光的看法[③]，虽说我

---

① 《回忆录》（1881）是托马斯·卡莱尔死后出版的自传体作品，表现出了卡莱尔严厉、阴郁、挑剔的一面。

② 查尔斯·金斯利（1819—1875），英国国教的一位泛教会牧师、大学教授、社会改革家、历史学家、小说家和诗人。他与工人学院组建劳动合作社，虽然都失败了，但鼓励了后来的工作改革。

③ 德国文学家兼科学家歌德（1749—1832）在1810年发表了长达1400页的论文质疑牛顿关于光、颜色和光谱的观点的有效性。因为歌德曲解了一些实验，因此他错误地指责了牛顿。

坚持认为可行，可他还是冷笑。他认为，让任何人都关心冰川移动是快是慢，还是根本不动，是一件非常荒谬的事情。据我判断，我从未见过头脑如此不适应科学研究的人。

在伦敦生活期间，我尽可能定期参加几个科学团体的会议，并担任了地质学会的秘书。但是，要在学会任职和定期出席活动，我的健康状况并不允许，我和家人决定住到乡村，我们都喜欢乡村生活，而且从来没有后悔过。

第 6 章

唐恩村的生活

在萨里郡和其他地方几次搜寻无果后，我们在唐恩村找到了房子并买下了它。我对这里白垩区特有植被的多样性感到满意，这与我在英格兰中部地区所习惯的一切大不相同；同时，我对这个地方的极度宁静和质朴更为满意。然而，这并不像一位德国期刊作家所说的那样是一个僻静的地方，他还说只有走骡道才能到我家！我们在这里自给自足，某种程度上来说也得到了令人满意的回馈，那便是，我们的孩子很方便经常来看我们，这也是我们没有预料到的。

很少有人能过着比我们更隐居的生活。我们除了短暂地拜访亲戚朋友，偶尔去海边或其他地方，也无处可去。在我们居住的第一阶段，我们稍微融入了社会，并在这里接待了一些朋友；但我几乎总是因为兴奋、剧烈颤抖和呕吐发作而使身体状况每日愈下。因此，多年来，我不得不放弃所有的晚宴；这对我来说是一种剥

这是达尔文故居庭院里的一条小路。达尔文经常沿着这条小路散步，锻炼身体。他称之为"思考之路"。图片版权已进入公有领域

夺，因为这样的聚会总是让我兴高采烈。出于同样的原因，我在这里只能邀请极少数科学界的熟人。

我一生中主要的乐趣和唯一的工作是科研。这样的工作带来的兴奋让我暂时忘却了，或者说赶走了我日常的身体上的不适。因此，在我的余生中，除了出版几本书之外，我没有什么可记录的。也许值得一提的是它们的出版的细节。

第 7 章

《物种起源》及其他作品

1844 年年初，我发表了我在"小猎犬"号航行期间对火山岛的观察结果 ①。1845 年，我不辞辛苦地修订了我的《研究日志》的新版 ②，最初它是菲茨罗伊 1839 年出版作品的一部分，这是我的第一部作品，该书的成功比其他任何一本书都更能让我自豪，直到今天，这本书在英国和美国的销量一直稳定，并已被翻译成德语、法语及其他语言。一本游记，尤其是一本科学游记，在出版多年后取得如此成功，令人惊讶。第二版在英国已售出 1 万册。1846 年，我的《南美洲地质观测》出版了。我经常会为自己的书写点日记，我的三本地质书（包括《珊瑚礁》）花了我四年半的

---

① 本书第 4 章提及的《火山岛地质观测》，1876 年该书再版时把《南美洲地质观测》也编入，书名统称《地质观测》。

② 本书第 3 章提到 1845 年出版的《环球航行期间访问的国家的博物和地质研究日志》(*Journal of Researches into the Geology and Natural History of the various countries visited by H.M.S. Beagle*)，该书是著名的《"小猎犬"号航海记》的前身。

1. Geospiza magnirostris.
2. Geospiza fortis.
3. Geospiza parvula.
4. Certhidea olivacea.

鸟类学家约翰·古尔德为达尔文 1845 年版《环球航行期间访问的国家的博物和地质研究日志》所作的插图，实物存于剑桥大学动物博物馆。图片版权已进入公有领域

时间。"我回到英国已经十年了，这期间因病耽误了多少时间？"关于这三本书，我没有太多可说的，只是对应社会呼声新版了很惊讶。（《地质观测》，1876年第 2 版；《珊瑚礁》，1874 年第 2 版）

　　1846 年 10 月，我开始研究蔓足下纲①的动物。在

──────────

① *Cirripedia*，节肢动物门甲壳亚门颚足纲鞘甲亚纲蔓足下纲，1834 年由德国和阿根廷的动物学家赫尔曼·伯迈斯特（1807—1892）命名。常见的蔓足动物有藤壶和茗荷。

智利海岸上，我发现了一种形态非常奇特的蔓足类，它会在似鲍罗螺[①]的壳上钻孔，与其他蔓足类区别很大，我只好把它单独分为一个亚目。最近，在葡萄牙海岸上又新发现了一个类似的属也钻孔。为了解我新发现的蔓足动物结构，我必须研究和解剖许多常见的蔓足类，这让我逐渐了解了整个类群。在接下来的 8 年里，我一直在研究这个课题，最终出版了两本厚的书（由雷学会[②]出版）。书中描述了所有已知的现存物种，并在两本薄的四开本中介绍了灭绝的物种。我十分确信 E. 布尔沃 - 利顿爵士[③]在他的一部小说里写的一位朗教授就是以我为原型的。朗教授写过两大卷关于帽贝的文章。

---

① *Concholepas*，骨螺科的似鲍罗螺属，目前为单型属，英语最早称其为"智利鲍鱼"（Chilean abalone），该属在法国医生、动物学家让·纪尧姆·布鲁吉埃（1749—1798）的作品中最早出现，法国博物学家拉马克于 1801 年正式定义。

② 雷学会（1844 年至今），专注于出版博物学书籍的学会，由医生、博物学家乔治·约翰斯顿成立，以纪念杰出的博物学约翰·雷（1628—1705）在动植物分类学上的突出贡献。达尔文在该学会出版过两本蔓足下纲的书。

③ 爱德华·布尔沃－利顿，第一代利顿男爵（1803—1873），英国作家和政治家，其小说在当时收获一定反响，并创造了"底层民众"（the great unwashed）、"笔尖胜过干戈"（the pen is mightier than the sword）等俗语。达尔文提到的"朗教授"出自其 1858 年出版的小说《他会用它做什么？》（*What Will He Do With It?*）。

虽然研究了这个类群8年，但据我日记的记载，其中大约有两年的时间因病没有进行研究记录。因为病情的原因，我在1848年去墨尔文做了几个月的水疗①，这对我很有帮助，回家后就能继续工作了。同年11月13日我父亲去世，同样因为疾病，我的健康状况很差，导致我不能参加父亲的葬礼，也不能作为他的遗嘱执行人之一。

我认为我的蔓足类研究有巨大的价值，且不说我描述了几种新的、不同寻常的物种形态，我还找出了不同类群器官的同源性②——我发现了黏着器官③，尽管在黏腺的研究上走了不少弯路；最后我还证明了在某些属中存在着微小雄性，与雌雄同体互补并寄生于雌雄同体上。虽然一次有位德国作家认为我的观点全凭想象，但

① 此处的"水疗"指爱丁堡大学医学博士詹姆斯·曼比·古利（1808—1883）在英格兰伍斯特郡的温泉小镇墨尔文开设的多家水疗诊所，此人和达尔文一样都是1825年成为爱丁堡大学的医学生。当时水疗在英国风靡。
② "同源性"这一生物学概念是指不同类群生物在某些器官在基本结构、生物体的相互关系以及胚胎发育的过程上彼此相同，因为可能有共同祖先。如脊椎动物的前肢，蝙蝠和鸟类的翅膀、灵长类动物的手臂、鲸鱼的前鳍以及狗和鳄鱼等四足脊椎动物的前肢，可能都是同源器官，都来自同一个四足动物祖先。自15世纪以来，这一概念在生物学研究中逐步走向深入。
③ 黏着器官及后面提到的"黏腺"都是指生物发展出吸附在物体表面的器官，黏腺可分泌黏液，幼体靠此固着系统吸附在物体表面，再行变态。达尔文在蔓足类动物中发现了这类器官。

达尔文 1854 年肖像，美国《哈珀杂志》（*Harper's Magazine*）1884 年 10 月版的插图，拍摄者为亨利·莫尔和约翰·福克斯，也是弗朗西斯·达尔文的 1887 年版《达尔文自传》的卷首插图。图片已进入公有领域

后一项发现最终得到了充分的证实。蔓足类动物高度多样性使得种群分类十分艰难，但当我必须在《物种起源》中讨论自然分类的原则时，蔓足类研究工作对我的巨大价值就显现出来了。不过我还是怀疑这项工作是否值得花费这么多时间①。

　　从 1854 年 9 月起，我把全部时间都花在整理我那

① 这句话的一种解释是因为当时科学家对蔓足类动物的研究的命名都自成一派，因而做的大多工作也不被理解或很容易被推翻。

一大堆笔记，花在观察物种演化[1]和进行相关的实验上。在"小猎犬"号的航行中，有好些东西令我印象非常深刻，我在南美潘帕斯草原的地层中发现的大型动物化石有着像现在的犰狳一样的护甲；其次，从南美洲大陆南下，我们发现十分相近的动物会交替出现；再次，加拉帕戈斯群岛（科隆群岛）的大多数岛屿上的物种都具有南美洲的特色，但各岛屿物种又略有不同，各有特点；从地质学的角度来看，这些岛屿却似乎都不是非常古老。

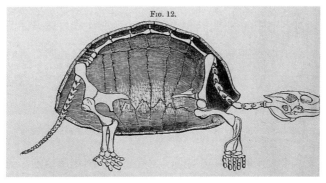

达尔文故居藏书中的休·福尔克纳于1868年出版的《古生物学手记》中的绘图。图片版权已进入公有领域

---

[1] 本部分中提到的演化，英文原词为"Transmutation"，该词最初为炼金术用语，19世纪初被引入生物学概括物种的变化，由于该词的定义存在一定争议，因而后来没有广泛使用。

很明显，像这样的事实，以及许多其他事实，只能用物种逐渐演化的假设来解释。这个问题一直困扰着我。但同样明显的是，各种生物找到完美适应生存习惯的案例数不胜数，无论是环境条件的作用，还是生物体本身（尤其是植物）的意志，都不能完全解释这些现象。例如啄木鸟啄树，或树蛙爬树，或是种子用钩状或羽状结构传播。我一直对这种适应感到非常震惊，如果这些都还没能解释，我认为试图用间接证据证明物种进化，几乎是毫无意义的。

回到英国后，我发现，如果我效仿莱尔《地质学原理》一书中的例子，收集所有与人为驯化和自然条件下的动植物变化有关的例子，也许就能对整个问题有所启发。我的第一本笔记于 1837 年 7 月开启[1]。我真正以培根原则[2]为基础，在没有任何理论的情况下，通过调查问卷、与经验丰富的饲养员和园丁交谈，以及广泛阅读，来大量收集事实依据，尤其是关于驯化产物的。当

---

① 本书第 4 章提到的《物种起源》写作的笔记本，名字叫作"Trans-mutation of Species"（"物种的演化"）。

② 培根原则，英国哲学家、现代科学的奠基人之一弗朗西斯·培根（1561—1626）提出的一种研究方法，也称"排除归纳法"，首先对需求进行描述，以指导系统、细致的观察。这样的观察对于提供高质量的事实论据是非常有必要的。然后，使用归纳法，即从一组事实论据归纳成一个或多个原理。

我看到我阅读过的和摘录过的各种书籍清单，包括整个系列的期刊和学报时，我对自己的努力感到惊讶。我很快意识到，选择才是人类成功为自身创造有用的动植物种群的基石。但如何将这种选择机制用于解释在自然状态下生存的生物体，在一段时间里对我来说仍然是个谜。

1838 年 10 月，也就是我开始进行系统调研的 15 个月后，我在消遣时偶然读到了马尔萨斯的《人口论》①，我充分准备好长期观察动植物生存习性，尽我所能理解其无处不在的生存竞争；我立刻意识到，在这种环境下，有利的变异往往会被保留，而不利的变异往往会被消灭。结果便是新物种的形成。至此，我终于有了一个行得通的理论。但我为了避免偏见，决定暂时连最简短的梗概也不写。1842 年 6 月，我第一次满足了自己，用铅笔写了一篇仅 35 页的理论摘要。后来在 1844 年夏天被扩充到 230 页，直到现在我还保留着它的完整副本。

但当时我忽略了一个非常重要的问题；我很惊讶，

① 《人口论》（*An Essay on the Principle of Population*），1798 年匿名发表的书籍，后得知其作者为英国人口学领域学者托马斯·罗伯特·马尔萨斯（1766—1834）。该书以警告口吻试图证明，若人口数量以指数形式增长（如每 25 年翻一番）而粮食生产以线性增长的情况下，除非出生率下降，否则二者的差距将导致粮食匮乏和饥荒。

除了哥伦布的立蛋原理，我怎么会忽视这个问题和解决方案呢。这个问题是，从同一个种群演化而来的有机生物的行为偏好，在演化过程中，它们的特征会产生差异。它们的分化非常明显，所有物种可以归入属，属归入科，科归入亚目，等等；我还记得当时我坐在马车上路过的确切地点，记得我想到了这个理论时多么高兴。这是在我来了唐恩很久以后才想到的。解决方案正如我所相信的那样，所有占主导地位和增长型物种在繁衍后代上的改良，往往会适应生存环境的高度多样化，在大自然中遵循经济适用的发展原则。

早在 1856 年，莱尔就建议我把自己的观点详尽地写出来。我立刻开始行动，其篇幅是后来《物种起源》的三到四倍；但这还只是我所收集材料的一个梗概，这些篇幅也只占我工作总量的一半而已。但在 1858 年初夏，我的计划被打乱了。当时在马来群岛的华莱士先生①给我寄了一篇他的文章《论变种无限偏离原始类型的倾向》，这篇文章和我的理论完全一致。华莱士先生

① 阿尔弗雷德·拉塞尔·华莱士（1823—1913），英国博物学者、探险家、地理学家、人类学家和生物学家。华莱士因创立"自然选择"理论而著名，促使达尔文发表了自己的演化论理论。华莱士从 1854 年起在马来群岛做了 8 年的广泛的博物学田野调查，并在马来群岛确定了现在生物地理学中区分东洋区和澳大拉西亚区的分界线（华莱士线）。

表示，如果我觉得他的文章不错，可以把它送给莱尔审读。

在莱尔和胡克的要求下，我提供了一份《物种起源》手稿的摘要，以及一封 1857 年 9 月 5 日写给阿萨·格雷的信[①]。这些材料，连同华莱士的论文，发表在 1858 年《林奈学会会议记录》第 45 页[②]。起初我很不愿意这样做，因为我觉得华莱士先生可能会认为我这样做是不道德的，毕竟那时我不知道他的性情是多么慷慨和高尚。我的手稿摘要和给阿萨·格雷的信都写得很糟糕，也没有打算出版。另外，华莱士先生的文章表达极佳，语言也清楚。然而，这篇共同发表的文章却几乎没激发任何关注，我记得的唯一关注我们的是都柏林的霍

[①] 达尔文在 48 岁的时候给美国哈佛大学的著名植物学家阿萨·格雷（1810—1888）写信，信件中阐述了"自然选择"的理论。这位 19 世纪重要的美国植物学家著有《北美植物志》，经常与达尔文互通信件，之后发表论文集《达尔文主义》（*Darwiniana*），解释宗教和科学不一定相互排斥。

[②] 伦敦林奈学会，成立于 1887 年，存续至今，为 18 世纪启蒙运动的产物，是世界上现存最古老的生物学会，后文将简写为"林奈学会"。查尔斯·达尔文于 1854 年当选成员。1858 年由达尔文和华莱士共同撰写的"关于物种形成变种的趋势；以及通过自然选择手段使品种和物种永存"（On the Tendency of Species to form Varieties；and on the Perpetuation of Varieties and Species by Natural Means of Selection）在学会宣读。

顿教授[1]发表的评论。他的结论是，文章中提到的所有新的观点都是错的，而对的都是陈词滥调，现实是物种从未改变。这也说明，任何新的观点都需要进行相当详细的解释，才能引起公众的关注。

1858 年 9 月，在莱尔和胡克的强烈建议下，我开始着手写一卷关于物种演化的书，但经常因疾病中断，我短暂地到莱恩医生在摩尔公园建立的水疗中心[2]休养过一段时间。早在 1856 年，我就开始为我的手稿做全面摘要，历经十三个月零十天的辛苦工作，继续缩减了后一半的篇幅，终于完成改卷。1859 年 11 月，该书以"物种起源"为名出版。尽管后来的版本，在原版的基础上进行了大量的补充和修订，但基本保持了原样。

这无疑是我一生中最重要的作品，一经发表便大获成功。最小的第一版次 1250 册在出版当天全部售出，第二版次 3000 册也在不久之后售出。现在（1876 年）

---

① 塞缪尔·霍顿（1821—1897），爱尔兰都柏林医学博士和科学作家，在看到达尔文和华莱士论文的印刷版后，1859 年 2 月 9 日向都柏林地质学会发表的讲话中简短地攻击了该理论。

② 萨里郡法纳姆镇的摩尔公园，17 世纪哲学作家和讽刺作家乔纳森·斯威夫特的庄园，19 世纪成为水疗中心，达尔文遇见的医学学者爱德华·威克斯蒂德·莱恩（1823—1889），此人的家族与达尔文相互熟悉。

在英国已售出 16000 册；考虑到这本书晦涩难懂，这个销量已经是非常好的了。它已被翻译成几乎所有欧洲语言，甚至被翻译成西班牙语、波西米亚语、波兰语和俄语等语言。据伯德小姐说，它也被翻译成了日语[①]（伯德小姐说得不对，我从箕作[②]教授那里听说的——弗朗西斯·达尔文），并且已有相关研究。甚至有一篇希伯来语的文章也在讨论"物种起源"，认为这一理论是包含在《圣经旧约》中的！关于《物种起源》的评论数不胜数；有一段时间，我收集了所有出现在《物种起源》及我相关书籍上的，这些评论数量（不包括报纸评论）总计 265 条；但过了一段时间，我绝望地放弃了收集。许多关于这个主题的独立论文和书籍已经出现；在德国，每一两年就会出现一本关于"达尔文主义"的书目或参考文献。

我认为《物种起源》的成功，在很大程度上要归功于我很久以前写的两篇简明扼要的文章，并最终整理出了一篇更完善的手稿，它自身就是书的梗概。通过这种

[①] 此处"伯德小姐"人物生平不详，但《物种起源》最早引入日本的时间为 1896 年，达尔文去世后。

[②] 箕作佳吉（Mitsukuri Kakichi，1857—1909），日本海洋动物学家，耶鲁大学和约翰·霍普金斯大学博士，东京帝国大学理学院教授。

方式，我能够选择更加有吸引力的事实和结论。多年来，我还遵循一条黄金法则，即每当我发现出版物中的新事实、新观察或新思想，如果与我脑中的已有结论相悖，我就会立刻把它记下来。因为根据经验，这样的结论和想法，有时比赞同你的更易被遗忘。基于这个习惯，很少有人对我的观点提出异议，而我根本没有注意到，也没有试图回答这些异议。

人们有时会说，《物种起源》的成功证明了"这个问题还没有解决"，或者"人们已经开始准备解决这个问题"。我认为这都不是绝对正确的，因为我偶尔也会打探不少博物学家的观点，从来没有遇到过怀疑物种不变论① 的人。即使是莱尔和胡克，尽管他们会饶有兴趣地倾听我的观点，但他们似乎从来都不同意。我试过一两次向身边的聪明人解释我的"自然选择"说的是什么，但都显然失败了。什么是绝对正确的，在我看来，应该是博物学家将数不清的细致观察储存在头脑中，他们站在属于自己的位置，一旦听到任何理论，都能做充分解释。这本书成功的另一个因素便是它篇幅适中，这要归

① 物种不变论认为生物界的所有物种一经造成，就不再发生任何变化，即使有变化，也只能在该物种的范围内发生变化，是绝对不可能形成新的物种的。

功于华莱士先生的那篇文章的问世。如果我以 1856 年开始写作时的规模出版，这本书将是现今《起源》的四到五倍厚，没什么人会有耐心看的。

大约在 1839 年，我对"自然选择"这个理论就有了清晰的构想，但我一直推迟到 1859 年才发表，这期间我收获颇丰。我并没有因推迟发表而错失什么机会，也不在乎人们是把这独创性的观点归功于我，还是华莱士；他的文章无疑使这一理论更好接受。

我只在一个重要问题上被人抢占了先机，而这让我有点遗憾。那便是用冰期来解释为什么相同种类的植物和少数动物会同时出现在遥远的山顶和北极地区。这个观点的提出让我非常开心，因此我完整地阐述了这个观点。我相信胡克在 E. 福布斯[①] 的著名的专题学术论文集（地质考察学术论文集，1846）出版之前就读过它。我们稍有几处观点分歧，但我仍然认为我是对的。当然，我从来没有在出版物中提到我是独立提出这个观点的。

在《物种起源》的写作中，几乎没有什么比解释很

---

① 爱德华·福布斯（1815—1854），英国博物学家，他首次提出假设，认为冰河时期山地植物和动物的分布被压缩到下坡，一些海洋岛屿与大陆相连。达尔文在《物种起源》中还是将该发现归功于福布斯。

多纲物种在胚胎和成年后形态上的巨大差异，以及同一纲物种胚胎之间的相似之处，更能使我感到欣慰。在我的印象中，《物种起源》的早期评论中没有人注意到这一点。我记得我在给阿萨·格雷的信中表达了对此的惊讶。近年来，一些评论家把全部功劳都归功于弗里茨·缪勒[1]和海克尔[2]。毫无疑问，他们的研究比我的更全面，在某些方面也比我更为准确。关于这个问题，我的材料可写整整一章，我本应做更多的论述，但很明显我没能引起公众的注意。在我看来，如果有人成功发现我的内容，也应该得到所有的赞扬。

这让我不得不说，我的评论者几乎总是诚实待我，那些缺乏科学知识而不值得被注意的可忽略不计。我的观点经常被严重歪曲、强烈反对和嘲笑，但正如我所相信的那样，他们也就是诚实表态罢了。总的来说，我很确信我的作品被一次又一次地过度赞扬了。我很高兴我避免了争论，这要归功于莱尔。多年前，在谈到我的地质工作时，莱尔强烈建议我不要卷入争论中，

[1]　弗里茨·缪勒（1822—1897），德国生物学家，在生物学上创造了"缪勒拟态"这一概念。

[2]　恩斯特·海克尔（1834—1919），德国生物学家、博物学家、哲学家、艺术家，同时也是医生、教授。海克尔将达尔文的进化论引入德国并在此基础上继续完善了人类的进化论理论。

因为这几乎没有任何好处，只会浪费时间，并且影响心情。

每当我发现自己犯了错误，或者工作不完美，以及当我受到轻蔑的批评，甚至当我被高估到有些不好意思时，我曾无数次地安慰自己说："我已经尽我所能，尽善尽美地努力了，未必有人能做得比这更好。"我记得在火地岛的"成功湾"①，我在想（并且，我相信，我给家里写了封信，大致是说），没有比给博物学添砖加瓦更好的工作了。我已经尽最大努力了，批评家们爱怎么说就怎么说，他们是无法摧毁我的信念的。

在1859年的最后两个月里，我全神贯注地准备《物种起源》的第二版，并收到了大量信件。1860年1月1日，我开始整理《动物和植物在家养状态下的变异》②的笔记，但直到1868年初才出版。拖延的部分原因是我经常生病，其中一次病了7个月；另外一部分原因是我想发表一些当时我更感兴趣的题材文章。

1862年5月15日，我花费10个月时间撰写的一

---

① 成功湾，火地岛勒美尔海峡附近的海湾，命名源自西班牙王室支持加西亚·德·诺达尔船队南美洲航行时的一艘"成功女神"帆船。达尔文于1832年12月年登陆该地。
② 《动物和植物在家养状态下的变异》是达尔文1868年1月出版的图书。

本小书《兰科植物的受精》[1]出版了：大部分案例是在前几年慢慢记录积累起来的。1839 年夏天，以及是再先前的那个夏天（我想应该是），我被引导开始关注借助昆虫进行杂交受精的花，我从对物种起源的推测得出的结论来看，杂交在保持特定形态不变方面发挥了重要作用。于是，接下来的每个夏天，我都或多或少地关注这个主题。1841 年 11 月，在罗伯特·布朗的建议下，我购买并阅读了 C. K. 斯普壬格[2]的一本精彩著作《发现大自然的秘密》，这便极大地提高了我对兰科植物的兴趣。1862 年之前的几年里，我一直特别关注英国兰科的受精；在我看来，最好的办法是尽可能完整地整理出一篇关于这类植物的专著，而不是慢慢观察大量其他植物的授粉方式。

事实证明，我的决定是明智的；因为自从我的书出

---

① 达尔文的《论英国和外国兰科植物利用昆虫受精的各种方法，以及杂交的良好效果》（*On the Various Contrivances by Which British and Foreign Orchids Are Fertilised by Insects，and On the Good Effects of Intercrossing*），简称《兰科植物的受精》，1862 年出版，经修订于 1877 年再版，但至 1900 年只售出 6000 余册。

② 克里斯蒂安·康拉德·斯普壬格（1750—1816），德国的神学家、教师、著名博物学家。他在植物性别的研究上有较高建树。斯普壬格是第一位发现花的功能是吸引昆虫进行异花授粉的自然学家。查尔斯·达尔文复验了斯普壬格的发现，也使斯普壬格的研究得到关注。

版以来，出现了数量惊人的关于各种花的受精的论文和独立的著作：这些论文和著作都比我能做到的好很多。可怜的老斯普壬格，优秀的观点一直被人忽视，直到他去世多年后，人们才充分认识到了他的前瞻性。

同年，我在《林奈学会杂志》上发表了一篇论文《报春花属的两种形态，或二型条件》。在接下来的 5 年中，我又发表了 5 篇关于二型和三型植物[①]的论文。我认为，在我的科学生涯中，没有什么比弄清这些植物的结构更使我感到满足的了。我在 1838 年，也许是 1839 年，注意到黄亚麻[②]的花柱的二型性，起初我以为这只是一种没有意义的变化。但在研究报春花属（*Primula*）的常见种时，我发现只按这两种形式研究，则太过规律和固定。按这样我会几乎确信，黄花九轮草和欧报春[③]正在走向雌雄异株的道路，即一类短雌蕊植株和另外一类短雄蕊植株均有败育倾向。按照这种观点推测，植物的生存受到了考验。但是，当发现具有短雌蕊的花与来自短雄蕊的花粉受精后，产生的种子会比四种中其他任

① 此处的"二型""三型"指动植物两性上的不同形态，也称"两性异形""三态异形"，这种叫法主要用于植物生殖器官的研究。

② 黄亚麻，*Linum flavum*，亚麻属多年生植物，花五瓣，原产于欧洲中部和南部。

③ 这两种都是报春花属植物。

何一种授粉方式都多，败育理论就被推翻了。经过一些额外的实验之后，可以明显看出，这两种形态，虽然都是完美的雌雄同株，但彼此之间的关系几乎和普通动物两性之间的关系一样。我们在千屈菜属植物的研究中发现一个更神奇的例子，三种形式彼此之间有着相似的关系。后来我发现，两种形态相同的植物结合产生的后代，与两种形态不同植物结合产生的杂交后代，有着密切且神奇的相似之处。

1864 年秋，我写完了一篇关于"攀缘植物"的长篇论文，并把它寄给了林奈学会。写这篇论文花了我 4 个月的时间；但当我收到校样时，我身体状况不太好，我没办法很认真地进行反馈修订，一些观点表达得很模糊。这篇论文很少被人注意到，但在 1875 年，它被更正并作为单独的一本书出版时[1]，销量却很好。我是通过阅读阿萨·格雷 1858 年发表的一篇短文[2]才开始研究这个课题的。是他给我送来的种子。在培育一些植物时，

① 达尔文的《关于攀缘植物的运动和习惯》(*On the Movements and Habits of Climbing Plants*)，1865 年《林奈学会学报》第 9 卷以论文出版，1875 年以书籍出版，插图由查尔斯·达尔文二儿子乔治达尔文（1845—1912）绘制。
② "卷须缠绕的笔记"(Note on the coiling of tendrils)，美国艺术与科学学院学报 [*Proceedings of the American Academy of Arts and Sciences*，4（1857-60）：98-9]。

我对卷须和茎的旋转运动非常着迷和困惑，这些运动其实非常简单，尽管乍一看非常复杂。因此，我购买了各种其他种类的攀缘植物，并研究了整个课题。我被植物缠绕所吸引，不满于亨斯洛在他讲座中对植物缠绕的解释，即它们天生就有螺旋式上升的趋势。后来这种解释被证实是错误的。攀缘植物为保证杂交受精，一些适应性表现得像兰花一样精妙。

如前所述的《动物和植物在家养状态下的变异》，写作开始于1860年年初，但直到1868年年初才出版。这是一本大书，写作上花了我四年零两个月的辛苦劳动。本书呈现了我们对驯化产物的所有观察，以及从各种来源收集的大量的事实。在第二卷中，在我们目前的知识允许的范围内，讨论了变异、遗传等现象的原因和规律。书的最后，我给出了未作证实的泛生假说[①]。一个未经证实的假设几乎没有价值；但是，如果以后有人被引向观察，建立类似的假设，那么我的理论就能起到很大的帮助，因为这样可以把数量惊

---

① 达尔文的泛生假说，受先人泛生思想的影响，在动植物性状基因的遗传上提出假说，认为是有机小颗粒聚集在性腺中，为配子细胞提供遗传信息。由于1900年科学界新发现奥地利修道院士格里哥·孟德尔（1822—1884）的遗传定律（1865至1866年发表）的价值，泛生假说不再流行。

人的孤立的事实联系起来，并且使它们变得容易理解。1875 年，我花了不少工夫作了大量修订，出版了该书第二版。

我的《人类的由来》①出版于 1871 年 2 月。在 1837年或 1838 年，我一旦确信某种物种是易变异的产物，我就无法避免这样的信念：人类也必然受到同样的法则支配。因此，我收集了一些关于这个主题的笔记，只是为了满足自己的需要，很长一段时间内，我没有任何出版的打算。尽管在《物种起源》中从未讨论过任何特定物种的起源推导，但我认为，为了不让有名望的人指责我隐瞒自己的观点，最好是加上一句，通过这部作品"给人类的起源和人类的历史提供线索，照亮溯源之道"。如果我在没有任何证据的情况下夸夸其谈我对人类起源的看法，那对这本书的成功是百害而无一益的。

但是，当我发现许多博物学家完全接受物种演化的学说时，我觉得把我所拥有的笔记整理出来，发表一篇关于人类起源的专著是明智的。我更乐意这样做，因为

---

① 本书第 5 章注释提到的《人类的由来和性选择》(*The Descent of Man, and Selection in Relation to Sex*) 的缩写。

这给了我一个充分讨论性选择①的机会——一个我一直很感兴趣的话题。性选择，以及驯化物种的变异这两个主题，以及变异的原因和规律、遗传和植物的杂交，是我唯一能够完整地写出来的课题，以便能用上我所收集到的所有材料。《人类的由来》花费我3年的时间来写，但还像往常一样，有一部分时间是由于健康欠佳而浪费了，还有一部分时间被用在准备其他书的再版和其他次要的作品上。《人类的由来》的第二版在1874年出版，经过了大量修正。

我的书《人与动物的情感表达》②于1872年秋出版。在《人类的由来》一书中，我本打算只用一章来讨论这个问题，但当我把笔记整理出来时，我发现这些思想还是需要一部独立的专著来阐释。

---

① "性选择"，或"性择"是达尔文提出的演化生物学领域的概念。解释同一性别的个体（通常是雄性）对交配机会的竞争将促进性状的演化。同一物种的两个性别之间，通常有至少一个性别必须竞争取得有限的交配机会。由于个体间存在可遗传的差异，造成有的个体在竞争中较为成功，较为成功的个体将此差异给予后代，便造成性择演化。该思想最早见于前文提及1858年由达尔文和华莱士共同撰写，在林奈学会宣读的文章。
② 《人与动物的情感表达》（*Expression of the Emotions in Men and Animals*）是达尔文继《物种起源》和《人类的由来》之后的第三部进化论著作，更多探讨了心理学，本书大量使用照片和插画，是图书插画史上的一个重要里程碑。

我的第一个孩子出生于1839年12月27日，我马上便开始给他最初的各种表情做记录，当时我坚信，最复杂和精细的一丝表情都必然有一个渐进和本真的起源。第二年的夏天，也就是1840年，我读到C.贝尔爵士[1]研究表情的出色作品，这大大增加了兴趣，虽然我不完全同意他说的各种肌肉都是为表情而特别创造出来的。从那时起，我偶尔也关注这个话题，无论是关于人类还是我们驯养的动物。我的这本书销量很大，出版当日便卖出5267册。

1860年夏天，我在哈特菲尔德闲逛、休整，那里大量存在着有两种茅膏菜属植物。我注意到许多昆虫被它们的叶子困住了。我带了一些植物回家，在给它们喂虫子时，我看到植物的须在动，这使我想到，植物捕捉这些昆虫可能是为了某种特殊的目的。幸运的是，我想到了一个关键的测试，那就是把大量的叶子放在多种密度相等的含氮液体和非含氮液体中；我发现只有前者才能激发植物的明显运动，这很明显是一个值得研究的新领域。

---

[1] 查尔斯·贝尔爵士（1774—1842），苏格兰医生、解剖学家、生理学家、艺术家，以发现感觉神经与运动神经的差异而知名。著有《剖析绘画表情的研究》（*Essays on the Anatomy of Expression in Painting*）。

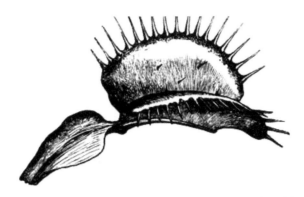

《食虫植物》中的插图，图片由弗朗西斯·达尔文和乔治·达尔文绘制。图片版权已进入公有领域

　　在后来的几年里，只要有空闲，我就继续做实验，我的《食虫植物》[①]一书于 1875 年 7 月出版，距我第一次观察已有 16 年了。这本书的迟来，就像我的其他几本书一样，给我带来了极大的好处；因为一个人经过长时间的停顿后，批判自己的作品就如同批判他人的作品。事实便是，植物受到适当的刺激时，会分泌一种含有酸和酵素的液体，可类比于动物的消化液，这无疑是一项了不起的发现。

　　在 1876 年的这个秋天，我发表了《植物界异花受

---

① 《食虫植物》(*Insectivorous Plants*) 是达尔文自然选择理论的又一著作，特别关注使它们能够在困难条件下生存的适应性。书中有达尔文本人，以及他的儿子乔治和弗朗西斯的插画。

精和自花受精的效果》[1]，成为《兰科植物的受精》一书的补充。在那本书中，我展示了异花受精的方法是多么完美，在这里我将展示结果是多么重要。在 11 年的时间里，我在研究中做了大量的实验，记录在这本书中，仅仅是偶然的观察；的确，要把这个偶然重复一遍，我才会彻底注意到一个显著的事实：自花受精的幼苗，甚至在第一代的高度和活力上，都不如异花受精的幼苗。我当时还希望修订出版我关于兰科的书，还有我二型和三型植物的论文，以及一些我从来没有时间整理的相关观点的更多观察。到那时，我的力气可能会耗尽，我将准备好大喊一声"恕我离去"[2]。

① 达尔文的《植物界异花受精和自花受精的效果》(*The Effects of Cross and Self Fertilisation in the Vegetable Kingdom*)，这本书可算是近亲繁殖研究的起点。
② 原文为拉丁语"Nunc dimittis"，《新约》路加福音拉丁手抄本中，耶路撒冷"正义而虔诚"的臣民西面（Simeon），在耶稣降临后发表了一段祈祷文，开头便是"现在你确实让你的仆人离去了，主啊"（Nunc dimittis servum tuum，Domine）暗示耶稣受难。

第 8 章

研究方法总结

我的《异花受精和自花受精的效果》于 1876 年秋出版；我相信，书中大大小小的结论，都指向奇妙而无尽的安排，即花粉在不同株的同类植物间传播。然而我现在认为，基于赫尔曼·穆勒[①]的观察，我本应更强烈地坚持自花受精的许多适应性，尽管我很清楚有很多这样的变化。1877 年我的《兰科植物的受精》增订版出版。

同一年，《同种植物上不同形态的花》[②]问世了，1880 年又出了第二版。这本书主要包括在林奈学会最初发表的几篇关于花柱异长的论文，经过修正，添加了许多新的内容，以及对同一植物开两种花的一些其他情况的观察。如前所述，没有哪项重大发现能比解密花柱

[①] 海因里希·路德维希·赫尔曼·穆勒（1829—1883），德国植物学家，他为达尔文的进化论提供了重要证据。

[②] 达尔文的《同种植物上不同形态的花》(*The Different Forms of Flowers On Plants of the Same Species*)，该书使用了瑞典植物学家林奈（1707—1778）的植物形态分类，1877 年出版，1880 年再版。

异长的含义给我带来如此前所未有的快乐。我认为，以反常规的方式杂交这些花朵的结果是非常重要的，因为它与杂交的不育性有关；虽然这些结果只有少数人注意到。

1879 年，我出版了恩斯特·克劳斯博士的《伊拉斯谟·达尔文生平》[①]的译文，并根据我所掌握的材料，补充了关于他性格和习惯的描写。许多我见过的人都对这种小生活细节的书很感兴趣，但令我惊奇的是，这书只卖了八九百本。

1880 年，在（我儿子）弗朗西斯·达尔文的协助下，我们的《植物运动的力量》出版了。这是一项艰巨的工作。这本书与我那本关于"攀缘植物"的小书[②]有某种相似之处，正如那本《异花受精和白花受精的效果》与《兰科植物的受精》也有几分相似；因为根据进化原理，除非所有种类的植物都具有某种类似攀缘植物的轻微运动能力，否则就不可能解释攀缘植物是如何在如此众多的不同群体中发展起来的。我证明确实如此；

---

① 又称《伊拉斯谟·达尔文传》，查尔斯·达尔文爷爷的生平传记，德国生物学家恩斯特·克劳斯（1839—1903）于 1879 年出版德语版，同年由查尔斯·达尔文及其家族成员完成英文版的翻译和修订。
② 本书第 7 章提到的《关于攀缘植物的运动和习惯》。

我进一步得到了一个相当广泛的概括，即由光、引力等激发的各种显著而重要的运动，都是基本的回旋运动[①]的变体。我总是乐于把植物拔高到有组织的生物来评价；因此，我特别乐意展示植物根尖有多少令人钦佩的适应性动作。

我现在（1881年5月1日）已经把一本题为"蚯蚓活动下植物沃土的形成"[②]的手稿寄给了印刷商。这是一个无关紧要的问题；我不知道这本书是否会引起读者的兴趣（从1881年11月到1884年2月，共售出8500本），但我很感兴趣。它完成了四十多年前在地质学会面前读过的一篇短文，复活了我旧时在地质方面的想法。

我已经提到了所有我出版过的书，这些都是我生命中的里程碑，就不再赘述了。在过去的三十年里，我发现自己的思考能力没有太大变化，除了我的脑子有些衰退。但是我的父亲活到83岁时，他的头脑仍然像以前

① 植物学领域中植物在生长过程中呈现绕轴转的圆周运动，达尔文将该运动解释为植物为适应周遭环境而进行的内生运动，如今依旧是普遍接受的解释。

② 《蚯蚓活动下植物沃土的形成：通过观察其习性》（*The Formation of Vegetable Mould Through the Action of Worms, with Observations on their Habits*），1881年10月（有幸赶在达尔文逝世前）出版，系达尔文最后一部学术专著，该理论发端于"小猎犬"号航行回归后对动物改造地质作用的进一步研究（1837—1838），详见本书第5部分。

一样活跃，他的所有身体机能都没有减弱；我希望在我的头脑丧失理智之前死去。我想我在猜测正确的解释和设计实验测试方面变得更熟练了；但这可能只是实践的结果，也可能是知识积累的结果。我还是像以前一样难以简明扼要地表达自己的意思。这种困难使我浪费了很多时间；但它也为我打开了一扇窗，那便是迫使我长时间、全神贯注地思考每一个句子，因此我被引导着通过推理自己或别人的观察去发现错误。

在我的头脑中似乎有一种宿命，使我一开始就把我的陈述或命题用错误或尴尬的形式表述出来。以前，我

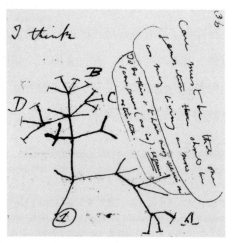

达尔文 1837 年的笔记本 "Transmutation of Species" 中的部分内容，主要描述物种的进化方式。图片版权已进入公有领域

在把句子写下来之前会先思考，但这几年来，我发现用我可怜的手尽快而潦草地写出一整页，把字都缩写一半，可以节省时间。然后精心纠正。这样草草写下的句子往往比我原来一笔一画写出来的更好。

关于我的写作方式，我已经说了这么多，我要补充的是，我在写大部头的书时，花了大量的时间来研究事情的总体安排。我先用两三页纸写出最粗略的提纲，然后再用几页纸写出较大的提纲，用几个词或一个词代表整个论述或一系列事实。在我开始摊开写作之前，每一个标题都会被填充或转化。正如在我的几本书中，其他人观察到的事实被广泛援引，由于我手头总是有几个完全不同的主题要写，我还想说我把三四十个大的档案夹贴好标签，放在多层陈列书柜里，我可以立即整理出一个独立的参考文献或备忘录。我买了许多书，在书的末尾，我把与我的工作有关的所有事实编成索引；或者，如果这本书不是我的，那就另写一份摘要，这样的摘要我有满满一抽屉。在开始任何主题之前，我会查看所有简短的索引，并制定一个通用的分类索引，通过抽出一个或多个适合的档案夹，这样我毕生收集的所有信息随时可用。

我曾说过，在过去二三十年里，我的思想在某一方面已经改变了。三十岁及以后，我读过许多诗歌，如弥尔顿、格雷、拜伦、华兹华斯、柯勒律治和雪莱的作品，感到非常愉快。甚至在我还是学生的时候，我就对莎士比亚的作品，尤其是历史剧，产生了浓厚的兴趣。我也曾说过，以前绘画给了我很大的乐趣，音乐也是。但这几年，我连欣赏一首诗都没法做到。最近我试着读莎士比亚的诗，发现它枯燥得令人难以忍受，使我作呕。我也几乎失去了对绘画和音乐的品味。音乐通常会让我过多地思考我正在做的事情，而不是给我带来快乐。我对美丽的风景仍有一定的鉴赏力，但它不再像以前那样给我带来美妙的快乐了。另一方面，小说，虽然地位不是很高，但作为想象的作品，多年来一直是我的一种奇妙慰藉和满足，我经常祝福所有的小说家。我能出声阅读的作品多到惊人，只要还算合理适度，只要结局不是不幸或不按该有的方向发展，我都喜欢。一部小说，按照我的品味，除非里面有一个人我能彻底地喜欢（如果是一个漂亮的女人就更好了），否则就不属于一流。

这种对高级审美趣味的丧失，令人琢磨不透而又惋惜，但又是最奇怪的，因为历史、传记和游记（不考虑他们可能包含任何科学事实），以及各种主题的随笔，都一如既往地使我感兴趣。我的头脑似乎已经变成了一种机器，从大量的事实中提炼出一般的规律，但我无法想象，为什么这会导致大脑一部分萎缩，而这部分又管理着我更高的品味。我想，一个头脑比我更有条理或架构得更好的人，是不会这样痛苦的；如果我能重新开始我的生活，我得制定一个规则，每周至少读一次诗，听一次音乐；因为也许我大脑现在萎缩的那部分可以通过使用而保持活跃。失去这些爱好就等于失去了幸福，可能会损害我们的智力，更有可能损害我们的道德品质，因为这会败坏我们天性中情感的部分。

我的书在英国销量很大，被翻译成多种语言，并在国外发行了好几版。我曾听人说过，一件作品在国外的成功是对其持久价值的最好检验。我怀疑这是否值得信任；但以这个标准来衡量，我的名声应该还能持续几年。因此，试着分析我的成功所依赖的心理素质和条件可能是值得的；虽然我知道没有人能正确地做到这一点。

我没有像赫胥黎[①]这样的聪明人所具有的那种非凡

---

① 托马斯·亨利·赫胥黎（1825—1895），英国生物学家和人类学家，研究比较解剖学，曾以随船助理军医的身份随英国军舰赴东南亚和澳洲考察了 4 年。他也是伦敦林奈学会会员，1860 年因与教会辩论，捍卫达尔文的进化论，而被称为"达尔文的斗牛犬"，其 1893 年的一份讲稿于 1897 年由严复译为《天演论》。

AN APPALLING ATTEMPT TO MUZZLE THE WATCH-DOG OF SCIENCE.

《帕卡》(*PUCK*)杂志 1883 年 4 月刊上描绘赫胥黎的漫画，弗里德里希·格雷茨绘，图片标题为"试图让科学的看门狗闭嘴，多么可怕的做法"。图片已进入公有领域

而敏捷的理解力和机智表达。因此，我是一个蹩脚的评论家。一篇论文或一本书，初读时，通常会使我钦佩，只有经过深思熟虑后，我才察觉到它们的弱点。我理解一长串纯粹抽象思维的能力是非常有限的；因此，我不可能在形而上学或数学方面取得成功。我的记忆力广泛而模糊，只要模模糊糊地告诉自己曾观察到或读到过与

我得出的结论相反的东西，或与之相同的东西，就足以使我谨慎起来。过一段时间，我一般就能想起来到哪里去找我的权威解释了。从某种意义上说，我的记忆力是如此之差，以至于我对一个日期或一行诗的记忆从来没有超过几天。

有些批评我的人说："哦，他是一个很好的观察者，但他没有推理的能力！"我不认为这是真的，因为《物种起源》从头到尾是长篇论证，说服了不少有能力的人。没有推理能力的人是写不出这本书的。我有相当高的创造力、常识或判断力，就像每个相当成功的律师或医生都必须具备的那样，但我相信，这不是在拔高自己的水平。

从有利的一面来看，我认为自己有一方面优于普通人，即我擅长注意到容易被忽视的事物并仔细观察它们。我在观察和收集事实方面的勤劳已经达到了它该有的高度。更重要的是，我对自然科学的热爱一直是坚定而热烈的。

然而，这种纯粹的热爱，在很大程度上是由于我想要受到博物学家同行们的尊敬。我从年轻的时候起，就有一种强烈的愿望，想要理解或解释我所观察到的一切，也就是说，把所有的事实都放在一些普遍规律之下。这些原因加在一起，使我有耐心对任何无法解释的问题进行多年的反复斟酌。据我判断，我不是那种被人牵着鼻子走的人。一方面，我一直坚定地努力使我的思想自由，一旦事实证明与任何假设相反时，我就放弃假设，无论它多么令人喜爱（我一般都忍不住在问题上形成假设）。事实上，我别无选择，只能这样做，因为除了珊瑚礁的假说之外，我不记得有任何一个最初形成的假说没有在一段时间后被放弃或被大改。这自然使我对综合科学中的演绎推理产生了极大的不信任。但另一方面，我不是个持高度怀疑态度的人——我认为这种心态对科学的进步是有害的。对于一个从事科学研究的人来说，持怀疑态度是明智的，可以避免浪费大量的时间。但是我也遇到过不少这样的人，我敢肯定，他们经常因此而不敢做实验或观察，而这些实验或观察本来是可以直接或间接地被证明是有用的。

我将举例说明我所知道的最奇怪的情况。一位先生（我后来听说他是当地一位优秀的植物学家）从东部的县给我写信说，普通蚕豆的种子或豆子，今年到处都长在豆荚的外面，位置不对。我回信询问更多的情况，因为我不明白这是什么意思；但是很长一段时间我没有得到任何答复。然后我在两份报纸（一份在肯特郡，另一份在约克郡）上看到了这样的段落："今年的豆子都长错了地方。"所以我想，这么笼统的说法一定是有根据的。于是，我去找我的园丁，一个肯特郡的老人，问他有没有听说过，他回答说："哦，没有，先生，一定是搞错了，因为豆子只在闰年长错地方，而今年不是闰年。"我又问他，它们在平年和闰年是怎样生长的，但我很快发现，他对豆子在任何时候是怎样生长的都一无所知，但他还是坚持了自己的观点。

过了一段时间，我收到了第一个知情人士的来信，他非常抱歉地说，如果不是从几个聪明的农民那里听到了这个消息，他就不应该给我写信。但是后来他又跟他们每一个人交谈，没有一个人知道自己说的是什么意思。因此，如果一个没有明确观点的陈述确实可以被称为一种信仰，这种信仰几乎能在没有任何根据的情况下传遍了整个英格兰。

在我的一生中，我只知道三个故意伪造的陈述，其中一个可能是个骗局，然而（已经有好几个科学骗局了）出现在了美国农业杂志。它与在荷兰的不同的种类的牛属动物杂交育种的公牛有关（其中一些牛的杂交我碰巧知道是不产生后代的）。作者竟厚颜无耻地说该研究与我的观点相符，说我一直对他的结论的重要性加以钦佩。这篇文章是一家英国农业杂志的编辑在转载之前为征求我的意见寄给我的。

第二个例子是作者从报春花属的几个品种中培育出来的几个变种，尽管亲本植株被小心地保护起来，不让昆虫进入，但它们都自发地产生了大量的种子。这篇文章发表时，我还没有发现"花柱异长现象"[①]的含义，整篇文章一定是骗人的，或者是忽略了那些长相丑陋、恶心的昆虫的作用，把它们排除在外。

第三个案例更令人好奇：胡斯[②]在他关于"近亲结婚"的书中，发表了一位比利时作者的一些长篇摘录，这位作家声称，让兔子以最接近的近亲繁殖的方式生育好几代，没有造成任何有害的影响。这篇报道发表在一份相当重要的期刊上——《比利时皇家学会的期刊》。但我不得不感到怀疑，我也不知道为什么，只知道这居然没有任何偶然

---

① 花柱异长（heterostylism），指花形态存在多种差异，如报春花属植物有两种类型的花：一种类型具有较长的花柱和较短的雄蕊（"针"型），而另一种类型具有较短的花柱和较长的雄蕊（"线"型）。达尔文在1877年论证了花的异型与自交不亲和是有关的，只有异型花之间授粉才是成功的。
② 阿尔弗雷德·亨利·胡斯（1850—1910），英国藏书家。他出身于银行家庭，追随父亲亨利·胡斯对藏书的兴趣，并帮助创立了伦敦书目协会。其书《近亲的婚姻》（*The Marriage of Near Kin*）于1875年出版后存在学术严谨性的争议。

性，我在饲养动物方面的经验让我认为这是不可能的。

因此，我很犹豫地写信给范贝内登①教授，问他作者是否值得信赖。我很快就收到回信，协会十分震惊，发现整个论证都在造假。（鉴于书中已经公开的错误言论，胡斯先生后来在书中插入一张纸条中指正自己的依据，但那些书最后也没卖出去。）《华尔街日报》曾公开向这位作者提出质疑，要求他说出自己在进行实验时住在哪里；大量的兔子养在哪里；毕竟他的实验耗费了好几年的时间，但没从他身上得到答案。

我的习惯是有条不紊的，这对我的工作有很大的帮助。最后，我有足够的空闲时间不用自己挣钱糊口。我身体不好，尽管这简直毁了我好几年，却使我免于社交和娱乐的干扰。

因此，我作为一个科研人的成功无论达到什么程度，就我的判断而言，都是由复杂多样的心理素质和条件决定的。其中最重要的还是对科学的热爱，对一些主题的长期反思，对观察和收集的无限耐心，以及对发明和常识之间的恰当调配。由于我的能力不偏不倚，竟很大程度上影响了不少科研人对某些重要问题的认识，多么令人惊讶。

① 皮埃尔·约瑟夫·范贝内登（1809—1894），比利时动物学家和古生物学家。

达尔文生平年表

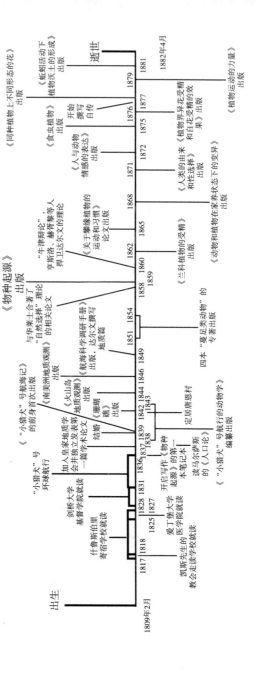

出生

1809年2月

凯斯先生走读学校就读
教会走读学校就读

1817 1818

什鲁斯伯里寄宿学校就读

1825

爱丁堡大学医学院就读

1827 1828

剑桥大学基督学院就读

1831

"小猎犬"号环球航行

1836 1837 1838 1839

加入皇家地质学会并独立发表第一篇学术论文
开始写作《物种起源》的第一本笔记
读马尔萨斯的《人口论》
结婚
《"小猎犬"号航行的动物学》编纂出版

《"小猎犬"号航海记》的前身首次出版

1842 1843 1844 1846

《南美洲地质观测》出版
《火山岛地质观测》出版
定居唐恩村
《珊瑚礁》出版

1849 1851 1854

《航海科学调研手册》出版，达尔文撰写地质篇
四本"蔓足类动物"的专著出版

《物种起源》出版

"与莱士合著了'自然选择'的相关论文

1858 1859 1860

"牛津辩论"，亨斯洛、赫胥黎等人捍卫达尔文的理论
《兰科植物的受精》出版

1862 1865 1868

《关于攀缘植物的运动和习惯》论文出版
《动物和植物在家养状态下的变异》出版

1871 1872 1875 1876 1877

《人类的由来和性选择》出版
《人类与动物情感的表达》出版
《食虫植物》出版
开始撰写自传
《植物界异花受精和自花受精的效果》出版

《同种植物上不同形态的花》出版

1879 1881 1882年4月

《蚯蚓活动下植物沃土的形成》出版
逝世

《植物运动的力量》出版

116

译者后记

时势造英雄，英国在维多利亚时期迎来了鼎盛的发展期，贸易的兴盛带来了社会的繁荣，蒸汽船可以进行环球航行、驶向未知的角落，世界的轮廓逐渐清晰，学术研究和学术交流有着良好的环境，各种思想碰撞出激烈的火花，催生出一大批勇于了解自然、发现自然规律的学者。查尔斯·达尔文便是生活在这样一个博采众长、迈向理性、学术高度繁荣的年代，前有生物分类学家卡尔·林奈、博物与进化学家让-巴蒂斯特·拉马克、政治经济学家托马斯·马尔萨斯等人，而他自身又和亚历山大·冯·洪堡、约翰·赫歇尔、罗伯特·布朗、弗朗西斯·高尔顿、查尔斯·巴贝奇等，从现在看来的科学奠基者有着或多或少的交集，从他的自传中我们能洞悉伟大时代造就的众多伟人。

在生物进化领域的伟人达尔文，其实在人生的早期也经历了类似于我们现代人的迷茫：他会因跟不上外语、数学的学习而苦恼，也会迫于家庭期望而去死记硬背每一项宗教信条，还会因为学习压力过大而对未来生涯感到迷茫，在年纪轻轻就感受到自己无法继承父业。但如果他的人生徘徊于此，便普通到不能再普通了。

然而他的人生却因一次近 5 年的航行而彻底改变。一艘英国皇家勘测舰的舰长召集一名随行学者，年少的达尔文在经历了家族内的反对和支持后，最终入选。从《自传》中可见，他多年后依旧清楚记得获得家族支持、入选"小猎犬"号环球航行时的喜悦。但实际的航行却是艰苦、难以适应的：晕船、失恋、船内的人际矛盾、船员的去世接踵而至，更是有很多地方是荒凉无人，连参考地图都少之甚少的。这看似绝望的环境却没能打败这个二十多岁的少年：他白天奔走在狭长的海岸及未知的内陆，收集对生物及地质地貌的发现，晚上撰写考察手记。除去海上度过的 18 个月，陆地上的实际考察时间有 3 年零 3 个月。

从达尔文的回忆录中，可以明确地看出"小猎犬"号航行在他人生中的伟大意义：大学期间从医学到神学再到博物学的涉猎只是充实了他的知识，而要真正拓宽自己的思考维度，还得是遵从自身兴趣、注重实地研究。达尔文便是这样在环球航行道上越走越清晰。他航行结束后的二十乃至三十年的研究、写作，都很大得益于这段宝贵的环球航行。由此可见，不凡的经历历练了他，使他变得伟大。

达尔文结束航行后在英国的生活趋于平静稳定，更确切地说，是一种踏实，他的研究整合与写作工作变多了，这恰是考验一位学者研究思路严谨性的重要环节，如果架构不稳，经验与实证不够坚定，《物种起源》及其他作品便是无稽之谈。达尔文对自己的发现做了严格的分类，排除错误，力争以客观实际为论据，为自己的研究建立起了空前宏观的地基。他以经济视角和物种竞争的观点引发对生态系统的思考，从动物对不同环境的适应情况丰富了进化学说；从不同物种的胚胎特质推测出物种的同源说；又从遗传与变异特质推断出泛生假说，完善了前人的研究。在这条研究途中，他碰到了很多与他一致的声音，这种"英雄所见略同"，已然是站在了更为科学的角度。

除此之外，达尔文身上，还有很多值得我们注意的点，例如他与人交往绝非人云亦云，或单纯追求物质上的交集，而是既能坚持自己正确的价值观，又能和而不同，或许这也是为什么他能与亨斯洛、莱尔、胡克、格雷、赫胥黎这样锲而不舍地追寻科学真理的人越走越近。达尔文也力求对自身及个人作品做出较为客观的评价，理解他人及公众对自身思想的看法，勇于承认自身错误。达尔文身体并非强壮，病痛时常折磨着他，但他更加珍惜来之不易的科研时光，从达尔文的自述，我们可看到一位一百多年前的科研人秉持的严谨务实。

本书为 1887 年查尔斯·达尔文之子弗朗西斯依据其父的手稿编定的删减版，而到了 1958 年，查尔斯·达尔文的孙女诺拉·巴洛出版了未删减版，相比本版，增加了 1860 年物种起源支持者与教会的在牛津大学的精彩辩论，感兴趣的读者可自行拓展阅读。

译者们在翻译过程中查阅大量史料，力求确切表达原文之意，对文化背景、专业术语作大量注释，更是幸而得到出版社编辑的指导，使译本在修改后得以完善。总而言之，尽管达尔文被我们熟知，但在翻译及查阅相关资料时，我们依旧被达尔文的生平所折服，切身感受到这是一本不可多得的佳作。

本书翻译具体分工如下：汪莉雅负责第第 1、3、5 章的翻译，黄群负责第 2、4、6 章的翻译，孙淼负责第 7、8 章的翻译，译者之间互相审阅，以求相互指正。由于译者水平有限，译文中肯定存在一些问题和不足，还请读者和专家批评、指正，不胜感激。

汪莉雅　黄　群　孙　淼
2023 年 2 月 28 日

The Autobiography of Charles Darwin

From *The Life and Letters of Charles Darwin*

Charles Darwin

Edited by Francis Darwin

My father's autobiographical recollections, given in the present chapter, were written for his children,—and written without any thought that they would ever be published. To many this may seem an impossibility; but those who knew my father will understand how it was not only possible, but natural. The autobiography bears the heading, "Recollections of the Development of my Mind and Character," and end with the following note:— "Aug. 3, 1876. This sketch of my life was begun about May 28th at Hopedene (Mr. Hensleigh Wedgwood's house in Surrey.), and since then I have written for nearly an hour on most afternoons." It will easily be understood that, in a narrative of a personal and intimate kind written for his wife and children, passages should occur which must here be omitted; and I have not thought it necessary to indicate where such omissions are made. It has been found necessary to make a few corrections of obvious verbal slips, but the number of such alterations has been kept down to the minimum.—F.D.

Chapter 1   The Beginning

A German Editor having written to me for an account of the development of my mind and character with some sketch of my autobiography, I have thought that the attempt would amuse me, and might possibly interest my children or their children. I know that it would have interested me greatly to have read even so short and dull a sketch of the mind of my grandfather, written by himself, and what he thought and did, and how he worked. I have attempted to write the following account of myself, as if I were a dead man in another world looking back at my own life. Nor have I found this difficult, for life is nearly over with me. I have taken no pains about my style of writing.

I was born at Shrewsbury on February 12th, 1809, and my earliest recollection goes back only to when I was a few

---

* 本章没有标题，为了阅读方便，编者加了此标题。为符合现在的英语习惯，对英文部分个别标点符号做了调整。

months over four years old, when we went to near Abergele for sea-bathing, and I recollect some events and places there with some little distinctness.

My mother died in July 1817, when I was a little over eight years old, and it is odd that I can remember hardly anything about her except her death-bed, her black velvet gown, and her curiously constructed work-table. In the spring of this same year I was sent to a day-school in Shrewsbury, where I stayed a year. I have been told that I was much slower in learning than my younger sister Catherine, and I believe that I was in many ways a naughty boy.

By the time I went to this day-school (Kept by Rev. G. Case, minister of the Unitarian Chapel in the High Street. Mrs. Darwin was a Unitarian and attended Mr. Case's chapel, and my father as a little boy went there with his elder sisters. But both he and his brother were christened and intended to belong to the Church of England; and after his early boyhood he seems usually to have gone to church and not to Mr. Case's. It appears ("St. James' Gazette", Dec. 15, 1883) that a mural tablet has been erected to his memory in the chapel, which is now known as the "Free

Christian Church.") my taste for natural history, and more especially for collecting, was well developed. I tried to make out the names of plants (Rev. W.A. Leighton, who was a schoolfellow of my father's at Mr. Case's school, remembers his bringing a flower to school and saying that his mother had taught him how by looking at the inside of the blossom the name of the plant could be discovered. Mr. Leighton goes on, "This greatly roused my attention and curiosity, and I enquired of him repeatedly how this could be done?" — but his lesson was naturally enough not transmissible. — F.D.), and collected all sorts of things, shells, seals, franks, coins, and minerals. The passion for collecting which leads a man to be a systematic naturalist, a virtuoso, or a miser, was very strong in me, and was clearly innate, as none of my sisters or brother ever had this taste.

One little event during this year has fixed itself very firmly in my mind, and I hope that it has done so from my conscience having been afterwards sorely troubled by it; it is curious as showing that apparently I was interested at this early age in the variability of plants! I told another little boy (I believe it was Leighton, who afterwards became a well-known lichenologist and botanist), that I could produce variously coloured polyanthuses and primroses by watering them with certain coloured fluids, which was of course a monstrous fable, and had never been tried by me. I may here also confess that as a little boy I was much given to inventing deliberate falsehoods, and this was always done for the sake of causing excitement. For instance, I once gathered much valuable fruit from my father's trees and hid it in the shrubbery, and then ran in breathless haste to spread the news that I had discovered a hoard of stolen fruit.

I must have been a very simple little fellow when I first went to the school. A boy of the name of Garnett took me into a cake shop one day, and bought some cakes for which he did not pay, as the shopman trusted him. When we came out I asked him why he did not pay for them, and he instantly answered, "Why, do you not know that my uncle left a great sum of money to the town on condition that every tradesman should give whatever was wanted without payment to any one who wore his old hat and moved [it] in a particular manner?" and he then showed me how it was moved. He then went into another shop where he was trusted, and asked for some small article, moving his hat in the proper manner, and of course obtained it without payment. When we came out he said, "Now if you like to go by yourself into that cake-shop (how well I remember its exact position) I will lend you my hat, and you can get whatever you like if you move the hat on your head properly." I gladly accepted the generous offer, and went in and asked for some cakes, moved the old hat and was walking out of the shop, when the shopman made a rush at me, so I dropped the cakes and ran for dear life, and was astonished by being greeted with shouts of laughter by my false friend Garnett.

I can say in my own favour that I was as a boy humane, but I owed this entirely to the instruction and example of my sisters. I doubt indeed whether humanity is a natural or innate quality. I was very fond of collecting eggs, but I never took more than a single egg out of a bird's nest, except on one single occasion, when I took all, not for their value, but from a sort of bravado.

I had a strong taste for angling, and would sit for any number of hours on the bank of a river or pond watching the float; when at Maer (The house of his uncle, Josiah

Wedgwood.) I was told that I could kill the worms with salt and water, and from that day I never spitted a living worm, though at the expense probably of some loss of success.

Once as a very little boy whilst at the day school, or before that time, I acted cruelly, for I beat a puppy, I believe, simply from enjoying the sense of power; but the beating could not have been severe, for the puppy did not howl, of which I feel sure, as the spot was near the house. This act lay heavily on my conscience, as is shown by my remembering the exact spot where the crime was committed. It probably lay all the heavier from my love of dogs being then, and for a long time afterwards, a passion. Dogs seemed to know this, for I was an adept in robbing their love from their masters.

I remember clearly only one other incident during this year whilst at Mr. Case's daily school,—namely, the burial of a dragoon soldier; and it is surprising how clearly I can still see the horse with the man's empty boots and carbine suspended to the saddle, and the firing over the grave. This scene deeply stirred whatever poetic fancy there was in me.

In the summer of 1818 I went to Dr. Butler's great school in Shrewsbury, and remained there for seven years still

Midsummer 1825, when I was sixteen years old. I boarded at this school, so that I had the great advantage of living the life of a true schoolboy; but as the distance was hardly more than a mile to my home, I very often ran there in the longer intervals between the callings over and before locking up at night. This, I think, was in many ways advantageous to me by keeping up home affections and interests. I remember in the early part of my school life that I often had to run very quickly to be in time, and from being a fleet runner was generally successful; but when in doubt I prayed earnestly to God to help me, and I well remember that I attributed my success to the prayers and not to my quick running, and marvelled how generally I was aided.

I have heard my father and elder sister say that I had, as a very young boy, a strong taste for long solitary walks; but what I thought about I know not. I often became quite absorbed, and once, whilst returning to school on the summit of the old fortifications round Shrewsbury, which had been converted into a public foot-path with no parapet on one side, I walked off and fell to the ground, but the height was only seven or eight feet. Nevertheless the number of thoughts which passed through my mind during this very short, but sudden and wholly unexpected fall, was astonishing, and seem hardly compatible with what physiologists have, I believe, proved about each thought requiring quite an appreciable amount of time.

Nothing could have been worse for the development of my mind than Dr. Butler's school, as it was strictly classical, nothing else being taught, except a little ancient geography and history. The school as a means of education to me was simply a blank. During my whole life I have been singularly incapable of mastering any language. Especial attention was paid to verse-making, and this I could never do well. I had many friends, and got together a good collection of old verses, which by patching together, sometimes aided by other boys, I could work into any subject. Much attention was paid to learning by heart the lessons of the previous day; this I could effect with great facility, learning forty or fifty lines of Virgil or Homer, whilst I was in morning chapel; but this exercise was utterly useless, for every verse was forgotten in forty-eight hours. I was not idle, and with the exception of versification, generally worked conscientiously at my classics, not using cribs. The sole pleasure I ever received from such studies, was from some of the odes of Horace, which I admired greatly.

When I left the school I was for my age neither high nor low in it; and I believe that I was considered by all my masters and by my father as a very ordinary boy, rather below the common standard in intellect. To my deep mortification my father once said to me, "You care for nothing but shooting, dogs, and rat-catching, and you will be a disgrace to yourself and all your family." But my father, who was the kindest man I ever knew and whose memory I love with all my heart, must have been angry and somewhat unjust when he used such words.

Looking back as well as I can at my character during my school life, the only qualities which at this period promised well for the future, were, that I had strong and diversified tastes, much zeal for whatever interested me, and a keen pleasure in understanding any complex subject or thing. I was taught Euclid by a private tutor, and I distinctly remember the intense satisfaction which the clear geometrical proofs gave me. I remember, with equal distinctness, the delight which my uncle gave me (the father of Francis Galton) by explaining the principle of the vernier of a barometer. With respect to diversified tastes, independently of science, I was fond of reading various books, and I used to sit for hours reading the historical plays of Shakespeare, generally in an old window in the thick walls of the school. I read also other poetry, such as Thomson's "Seasons," and the recently published poems of Byron and Scott. I mention this because later in life I wholly lost, to my great regret, all pleasure from poetry of any kind, including Shakespeare. In connection with pleasure from poetry, I may add that in 1822 a vivid delight in scenery was first awakened in my mind, during a riding tour on the borders of Wales, and this has lasted longer than any other aesthetic pleasure.

Early in my school days a boy had a copy of the "Wonders of the World," which I often read, and disputed with other boys about the veracity of some of the statements; and I believe that this book first gave me a wish to travel in remote countries, which was ultimately fulfilled by the voyage of the "Beagle". In the latter part of my school life I became passionately fond of shooting; I do not believe that any one could have shown more zeal for the most holy cause than I did for shooting birds. How well I remember killing my first snipe, and my excitement was so great that I had much difficulty in reloading my gun from the trembling of my hands. This taste long continued, and I became a very good shot. When at Cambridge I used to practise throwing up my gun to my shoulder before a looking-glass to see that I threw it up straight. Another and better plan was to get a friend to wave about a lighted candle, and then to fire at it with a cap on the nipple, and if the aim was accurate the little puff of air would blow out the candle. The explosion of the cap caused a sharp crack, and I was told that the tutor of the college remarked,"What an extraordinary thing it is, Mr. Darwin seems to spend hours in cracking a horse-whip in his room, for I often hear the crack when I pass under his windows."

I had many friends amongst the schoolboys, whom I loved dearly, and I think that my disposition was then very affectionate.

With respect to science, I continued collecting minerals with much zeal, but quite unscientifically—all that I cared about was a new-*named* mineral, and I hardly attempted to classify them. I must have observed insects with some little care, for when ten years old (1819) I went for three weeks to Plas Edwards on the sea-coast in Wales, I was very much interested and surprised at seeing a large black and scarlet Hemipterous insect, many moths (Zygaena), and a Cicindela which are not found in Shropshire. I almost made up my mind to begin collecting all the insects which I could find dead, for on consulting my sister I concluded that it was not right to kill insects for the sake of making a collection. From reading White's "Selborne," I took much pleasure in watching the habits of birds, and even made notes on the subject. In my simplicity I remember wondering why every gentleman did not become an ornithologist.

Towards the close of my school life, my brother worked hard at chemistry, and made a fair laboratory with proper apparatus in the tool-house in the garden, and I was allowed to aid him as a servant in most of his experiments. He made all the gases and many compounds, and I read with great care several books on chemistry, such as Henry and Parkes' "Chemical Catechism." The subject interested me greatly, and we often used to go on working till rather late at night. This was the best part of my education at school, for it showed me practically the meaning of experimental science. The fact that we worked at chemistry somehow got known at school, and as it was an unprecedented fact, I was nicknamed "Gas." I was also once publicly rebuked by the head-master, Dr. Butler, for thus wasting my time on such useless subjects; and he called me very unjustly a "poco curante," and as I did not understand what he meant, it seemed to me a fearful reproach.

As I was doing no good at school, my father wisely took me away at a rather earlier age than usual, and sent me (Oct. 1825) to Edinburgh University with my brother, where I stayed for two years or sessions. My brother was completing his medical studies, though I do not believe he ever really intended to practise, and I was sent there to commence them. But soon after this period I became convinced from various small circumstances that my father would leave me property enough to subsist on with some comfort, though I never imagined that I should be so rich a man as I am; but my belief was sufficient to check any strenuous efforts to learn medicine.

The instruction at Edinburgh was altogether by lectures, and these were intolerably dull, with the exception of those on chemistry by Hope; but to my mind there are no advantages and many disadvantages in lectures compared with reading. Dr. Duncan's lectures on Materia Medica at 8 o'clock on a winter's morning are something fearful to remember. Dr. — made his lectures on human anatomy as dull as he was himself, and the subject disgusted me. It has proved one of the greatest evils in my life that I was not urged to practise dissection, for I should soon have got over my disgust; and the practice would have been invaluable for all my future work. This has been an irremediable evil, as well as my incapacity to draw. I also attended regularly the clinical wards in the hospital. Some of the cases distressed me a good deal, and I still have vivid pictures before me of some of them; but I was not so foolish as to allow this to lessen my attendance. I cannot understand why this part of my medical course did not interest me in a greater degree; for during the summer before coming to Edinburgh I began attending some of the poor people, chiefly children and women in Shrewsbury: I wrote down as full an account as I could of the case with all the symptoms, and read them aloud to my father, who suggested further inquiries and advised me what medicines to give, which I made up myself. At one time I had at least a dozen patients, and I felt a keen interest in the work. My father, who was by far the best judge of character whom I ever knew, declared that I should make a successful physician,—meaning by this one who would get many patients. He maintained that the chief element of success was exciting confidence; but what he saw in me which convinced him that I should create confidence I know not. I also attended on two occasions the operating theatre in the hospital at Edinburgh, and saw two very bad operations, one on a child, but I rushed away before they were completed. Nor did I ever attend again, for hardly any inducement would have been strong enough to make me do so; this being long before the blessed days of chloroform. The two cases fairly haunted me for many a long year.

My brother stayed only one year at the University, so that during the second year I was left to my own resources; and this was an advantage, for I became well acquainted with several young men fond of natural science. One of these was

Ainsworth, who afterwards published his travels in Assyria; he was a Wernerian geologist, and knew a little about many subjects. Dr. Coldstream was a very different young man, prim, formal, highly religious, and most kind-hearted; he afterwards published some good zoological articles. A third young man was Hardie, who would, I think, have made a good botanist, but died early in India. Lastly, Dr. Grant, my senior by several years, but how I became acquainted with him I cannot remember; he published some first-rate zoological papers, but after coming to London as Professor in University College, he did nothing more in science, a fact which has always been inexplicable to me. I knew him well; he was dry and formal in manner, with much enthusiasm beneath this outer crust. He one day, when we were walking together, burst forth in high admiration of Lamarck and his views on evolution. I listened in silent astonishment, and as far as I can judge without any effect on my mind. I had previously read the "Zoonomia" of my grandfather, in which similar views are maintained, but without producing any effect on me. Nevertheless it is probable that the hearing rather early in life such views maintained and praised may have favoured my upholding them under a different form in my "Origin of Species." At this time I admired greatly the "Zoonomia;" but on reading it a second time after an interval of ten or fifteen years, I was much disappointed; the proportion of speculation being so large to the facts given.

Drs. Grant and Coldstream attended much to marine Zoology, and I often accompanied the former to collect animals in the tidal pools, which I dissected as well as I could. I also became friends with some of the Newhaven fishermen, and sometimes accompanied them when they trawled for oysters, and thus got many specimens. But from not having had any regular practice in dissection, and from possessing only a wretched microscope, my attempts were very poor. Nevertheless I made one interesting little discovery, and read, about the beginning of the year 1826, a short paper on the subject before the Plinian Society. This was that the so-called ova of Flustra had the power of independent movement by means of cilia, and were in fact larvae. In another short paper I showed that the little globular bodies which had been supposed to be the young state of Fucus loreus were the egg-cases of the wormlike

Pontobdella muricata.

The Plinian Society was encouraged and, I believe, founded by Professor Jameson: it consisted of students and met in an underground room in the University for the sake of reading papers on natural science and discussing them. I used regularly to attend, and the meetings had a good effect on me in stimulating my zeal and giving me new congenial acquaintances. One evening a poor young man got up, and after stammering for a prodigious length of time, blushing crimson, he at last slowly got out the words, "Mr. President, I have forgotten what I was going to say." The poor fellow looked quite overwhelmed, and all the members were so surprised that no one could think of a word to say to cover his confusion. The papers which were read to our little society were not printed, so that I had not the satisfaction of seeing my paper in print; but I believe Dr. Grant noticed my small discovery in his excellent memoir on Flustra.

I was also a member of the Royal Medical Society, and attended pretty regularly; but as the subjects were exclusively medical, I did not much care about them. Much rubbish was talked there, but there were some good speakers, of whom the best was the present Sir J. Kay-Shuttleworth. Dr. Grant took me occasionally to the meetings of the Wernerian Society, where various papers on natural history were read, discussed, and afterwards published in the "Transactions." I heard Audubon deliver there some interesting discourses on the habits of N. American birds, sneering somewhat unjustly at Waterton. By the way, a negro lived in Edinburgh, who had travelled with Waterton, and gained his livelihood by stuffing birds, which he did excellently: he gave me lessons for payment, and I used often to sit with him, for he was a very pleasant and intelligent man.

Mr. Leonard Horner also took me once to a meeting of the Royal Society of Edinburgh, where I saw Sir Walter Scott in the chair as President, and he apologised to the meeting as not feeling fitted for such a position. I looked at him and at the whole scene with some awe and reverence, and I think it was owing to this visit during my youth, and to my having attended the Royal Medical Society, that I felt the honour of being elected a few years ago an honorary member of both these Societies, more than any other similar honour. If I had been told at that time that I should one day have been thus honoured, I declare that I should have thought it as ridiculous and improbable, as if I had been told that I should be elected King of England.

During my second year at Edinburgh I attended — 's lectures on Geology and Zoology, but they were incredibly dull. The sole effect they produced on me was the determination never as long as I lived to read a book on Geology, or in any way to study the science. Yet I feel sure that I was prepared for a philosophical treatment of the subject; for an old Mr. Cotton in Shropshire, who knew a good deal about rocks, had pointed out to me two or three years previously a well-known large erratic boulder in the town of Shrewsbury, called the "bell-stone"; he told me that there was no rock of the same kind nearer than Cumberland or Scotland, and he solemnly assured me that the world would come to an end before any one would be able to explain how this stone came where it now lay. This produced a deep impression on me, and I meditated over this wonderful stone. So that I felt the keenest delight when I first read of the action of icebergs in transporting boulders, and I gloried in the progress of Geology. Equally striking is the fact that I, though now only sixty-seven years old, heard the Professor, in a field lecture at Salisbury Craigs, discoursing on a trapdyke, with amygdaloidal margins and the strata indurated on each side, with volcanic rocks all around us, say that it was a fissure filled with sediment from above, adding with a sneer that there were men who maintained that it had been injected from beneath in a molten condition. When I think of this lecture, I do not wonder that I determined never to attend to Geology.

From attending —— 's lectures, I became acquainted with the curator of the museum, Mr. Macgillivray, who afterwards published a large and excellent book on the birds of Scotland. I had much interesting natural-history talk with him, and he was very kind to me. He gave me some rare shells, for I at that time collected marine mollusca, but with no great zeal.

My summer vacations during these two years were wholly given up to amusements, though I always had some book in hand, which I read with interest. During the summer of 1826 I took a long walking tour with two friends with knapsacks on our backs through North wales. We walked thirty miles most days, including one day the ascent of Snowdon. I also went with my sister a riding tour in North Wales, a servant with saddle-bags carrying our clothes. The autumns were devoted to shooting chiefly at Mr. Owen's, at Woodhouse, and at my Uncle Jos's (Josiah Wedgwood, the son of the founder of the Etruria Works.) at Maer. My zeal was so great that I used to place my shooting-boots open by my bed-side when I went to bed, so as not to lose half a minute in putting them on in the morning; and on one occasion I reached a distant part of the Maer estate, on the 20th of August for black-game shooting, before I could see: I then toiled on with the game-keeper the whole day through thick heath and young Scotch firs.

I kept an exact record of every bird which I shot throughout the whole season. One day when shooting at Woodhouse with Captain Owen, the eldest son, and Major Hill, his cousin, afterwards Lord Berwick, both of whom I liked very much, I thought myself shamefully used, for every time after I had fired and thought that I had killed a bird, one of the two acted as if loading his gun, and cried out,"You must not count that bird, for I fired at the same time," and the gamekeeper, perceiving the joke, backed them up. After some hours they told me the joke, but it was no joke to me, for I had shot a large number of birds, but did not know how many, and could not add them to my list, which I used to do by making a knot in a piece of string tied to a button-hole. This my wicked friends had perceived.

How I did enjoy shooting! But I think that I must have been half-consciously ashamed of my zeal, for I tried to persuade myself that shooting was almost an intellectual employment; it required so much skill to judge where to find most game and to hunt the dogs well.

One of my autumnal visits to Maer in 1827 was memorable from meeting there Sir J. Mackintosh, who was the best converser I ever listened to. I heard afterwards with a glow of pride that he had said, "There is something in that young man that interests me." This must have been chiefly due to his perceiving that I listened with much interest to everything which he said, for I was as ignorant as a pig about his subjects of history, politics, and moral philosophy. To hear of praise from an eminent person, though no doubt apt or certain to excite vanity, is, I think, good for a young man, as it helps to keep him in the right course.

My visits to Maer during these two or three succeeding years were quite delightful, independently of the autumnal shooting. Life there was perfectly free; the country was very pleasant for walking or riding; and in the evening there was much very agreeable conversation, not so personal as it generally is in large family parties, together with music. In the summer the whole family used often to sit on the steps of the old portico, with the flower-garden in front, and with the steep wooded bank opposite the house reflected in the lake, with here and there a fish rising or a water-bird paddling about. Nothing has left a more vivid picture on my mind than these evenings at Maer. I was also attached to and greatly revered my Uncle Jos; he was silent and reserved, so as to be a rather awful man; but he sometimes talked openly with me. He was the very type of an upright man, with the clearest judgment. I do not believe that any power on earth could have made him swerve an inch from what he considered the right course. I used to apply to him in my mind the well-known ode of Horace, now forgotten by me, in which the words "nec vultus tyranni, etc.," come in.

(Justum et tenacem propositi virum

Non civium ardor prava jubentium

Non vultus instantis tyranni

Mente quatit solida.)

Chapter 2   Cambridge, 1828–1831

After having spent two sessions in Edinburgh, my father perceived, or he heard from my sisters, that I did not like the thought of being a physician, so he proposed that I should become a clergyman. He was very properly vehement against my turning into an idle sporting man, which then seemed my probable destination. I asked for some time to consider, as from what little I had heard or thought on the subject I had scruples about declaring my belief in all the dogmas of the Church of England; though otherwise I liked the thought of being a country clergyman. Accordingly I read with care "Pearson on the Creed," and a few other books on divinity; and as I did not then in the least doubt the strict and literal truth of every word in the Bible, I soon persuaded myself that our Creed must be fully accepted.

Considering how fiercely I have been attacked by the orthodox, it seems ludicrous that I once intended to be a clergyman. Nor was this intention and my father's wish ever formerly given up, but died a natural death when, on leaving Cambridge, I joined the "Beagle" as naturalist. If the phrenologists are to be trusted, I was well fitted in one respect to be a clergyman. A few years ago the secretaries of a German psychological society asked me earnestly by letter for a photograph of myself; and some time afterwards I received the proceedings of one of the meetings, in which it seemed that the shape of my head had been the subject of a public discussion, and one of the speakers declared that I had the bump of reverence developed enough for ten priests.

As it was decided that I should be a clergyman, it was necessary that I should go to one of the English universities and take a degree; but as I had never opened a classical book since leaving school, I found to my dismay, that in the two intervening years I had actually forgotten, incredible as it may appear, almost everything which I had learnt, even to some few of the Greek letters. I did not therefore proceed to Cambridge at the usual time in October, but worked with a private tutor in Shrewsbury, and went to Cambridge after the Christmas vacation, early in 1828. I soon recovered my school standard of knowledge, and could translate easy Greek books, such as Homer and the Greek Testament, with moderate facility.

During the three years which I spent at Cambridge my time was wasted, as far as the academical studies were concerned, as completely as at Edinburgh and at school. I attempted mathematics, and even went during the summer of 1828 with a private tutor (a very dull man) to Barmouth, but I got on very slowly. The work was repugnant to me, chiefly from my not being able to see any meaning in the early steps in algebra. This impatience was very foolish, and in after years I have deeply regretted that I did not proceed far enough at least to understand something of the great leading principles of mathematics, for men thus endowed seem to have an extra sense. But I do not believe that I should ever have succeeded beyond a very low grade. With respect to Classics I did nothing except attend a few compulsory college lectures, and the attendance was almost nominal. In my second year I had to work for a month or two to pass the Little—Go, which I did easily. Again, in my last year I worked with some earnestness for my final degree of B.A., and brushed up my Classics, together with a little Algebra and Euclid, which latter gave me much pleasure, as it did at school. In order to pass the B.A. examination, it was also necessary to get up Paley's "Evidences of Christianity," and his "Moral Philosophy." This was done in a thorough manner, and I am convinced that I could have written out the whole of the "Evidences" with perfect correctness, but not of course in the clear language of Paley. The logic of this book and, as I may add, of his "Natural Theology," gave me as much delight as did Euclid. The careful study of these works, without attempting to learn any part by rote, was the only part of the academical course which, as I then felt and as I still believe, was of the least use to me in the education of my mind. I did not at that time trouble myself about Paley's premises; and taking these on trust, I was charmed and convinced by the long line of argumentation. By answering well the examination questions in Paley, by doing Euclid well, and by not failing miserably in Classics, I gained a good place among the oi polloi or crowd of men who do not go in for honours. Oddly enough, I cannot remember how high I stood, and my memory fluctuates between the fifth, tenth, or twelfth, name on the list. (Tenth in the list of January 1831.)

Public lectures on several branches were given in the University, attendance being quite voluntary; but I was so sickened with lectures at Edinburgh that I did not even attend Sedgwick's eloquent and interesting lectures. Had I done so I should probably have become a geologist earlier than I did. I attended, however, Henslow's lectures on Botany, and liked them much for their extreme clearness, and the admirable illustrations; but I did not study botany. Henslow used to take his pupils, including several of the older members of the University, field excursions, on foot or in coaches, to distant places, or in a barge down the river, and lectured on the rarer plants and animals which were observed. These excursions were delightful.

Although, as we shall presently see, there were some redeeming features in my life at Cambridge, my time was sadly wasted there, and worse than wasted. From my passion for shooting and for hunting, and, when this failed, for riding across country, I got into a sporting set, including some dissipated low-minded young men. We used often to dine together in the evening, though these dinners often included men of a higher stamp, and we sometimes drank too much, with jolly singing and playing at cards afterwards. I know that I ought to feel ashamed of days and evenings thus spent, but as some of my friends were very pleasant, and we were all in the highest spirits, I cannot help looking back to these times with much pleasure.

But I am glad to think that I had many other friends of a widely different nature. I was very intimate with Whitley (Rev. C. Whitley, Hon. Canon of Durham, formerly Reader in Natural Philosophy in Durham University.), who was afterwards Senior Wrangler, and we used continually to take long walks together. He inoculated me with a taste for pictures and good engravings, of which I bought some. I frequently went to the Fitzwilliam Gallery, and my taste must have been fairly good, for I certainly admired the best pictures, which I discussed with the old curator. I read also with much interest Sir Joshua Reynolds' book. This taste, though not natural to me, lasted for several years, and many of the pictures in the National Gallery in London gave me much pleasure; that of Sebastian del Piombo exciting in me a sense of sublimity.

I also got into a musical set, I believe by means of my warm-hearted friend, Herbert (The late John Maurice Herbert, County Court Judge of Cardiff and the Monmouth Circuit.), who took a high wrangler's degree. From associating with these men, and hearing them play, I acquired a strong taste for music, and used very often to time my walks so as to hear on week days the anthem in King's College Chapel. This gave me intense pleasure, so that my backbone would sometimes shiver. I am sure that there was no affectation or mere imitation in this taste, for I used generally to go by myself to King's College, and I sometimes hired the chorister boys to sing in my rooms. Nevertheless I am so utterly destitute of an ear, that I cannot perceive a discord, or keep time and hum a tune correctly; and it is a mystery how I could possibly have derived pleasure from music.

My musical friends soon perceived my state, and sometimes amused themselves by making me pass an examination, which consisted in ascertaining how many tunes I could recognise when they were played rather more quickly or slowly than usual. "God save the King," when thus played, was a sore puzzle. There was another man with almost as bad an ear as I had, and strange to say he played a little on the flute. Once I had the triumph of beating him in one of our musical examinations.

But no pursuit at Cambridge was followed with nearly so much eagerness or gave me so much pleasure as collecting beetles. It was the mere passion for collecting, for I did not dissect them, and rarely compared their external characters with published descriptions, but got them named anyhow. I will give a proof of my zeal: one day, on tearing off some old bark, I saw two rare beetles, and seized one in each hand; then I saw a third and new kind, which I could not bear to lose, so that I popped the one which I held in my right hand into my mouth. Alas! it ejected some intensely acrid fluid, which burnt my tongue so that I was forced to spit the beetle out, which was lost, as was the third one.

I was very successful in collecting, and invented two new methods; I employed a labourer to scrape during the winter, moss off old trees and place it in a large bag, and likewise to collect the rubbish at the bottom of the barges in which reeds are brought from the fens, and thus I got some very rare species. No poet ever felt more delighted at seeing his first poem published than I did at seeing, in Stephens' "Illustrations of British Insects," the magic words, "captured by C. Darwin, Esq." I was introduced to entomology by my second cousin W. Darwin Fox, a clever and most pleasant man, who was then at Christ's College, and with whom I became extremely intimate. Afterwards I became well acquainted, and went out collecting, with Albert Way of Trinity, who in after years became a well-known archaeologist; also with H. Thompson of the same College, afterwards a leading agriculturist, chairman of a great railway, and Member of Parliament. It seems therefore that a taste for collecting beetles is some indication of future success in life!

I am surprised what an indelible impression many of the beetles which I caught at Cambridge have left on my mind. I can remember the exact appearance of certain posts, old trees and banks where I made a good capture. The pretty Panagaeus crux-major was a treasure in those days, and here at Down I saw a beetle running across a walk, and on picking it up instantly perceived that it differed slightly from P. crux-major, and it turned out to be P. quadripunctatus, which is only a variety or closely allied species, differing from it very slightly in outline. I had never seen in those old days Licinus alive, which to an uneducated eye hardly differs from many of the black Carabidous beetles; but my sons found here a specimen, and I instantly recognised that it was new to me; yet I had not looked at a British beetle for the last twenty years.

I have not as yet mentioned a circumstance which influenced my whole career more than any other. This was my friendship with Professor Henslow. Before coming up to Cambridge, I had heard of him from my brother as a man who knew every branch of science, and I was accordingly prepared to reverence him. He kept open house once every week when all undergraduates, and some older members of the University, who were attached to science, used to meet in the evening. I soon got, through Fox, an invitation, and went there regularly. Before long I became well acquainted with Henslow, and during the latter half of my time at Cambridge took long walks with him on most days; so that I was called by some of the dons "the man who walks with Henslow;" and in the evening I was very often asked to join his family dinner. His knowledge was great in botany, entomology, chemistry, mineralogy, and geology. His strongest taste was to draw conclusions from long-continued minute observations. His judgment was excellent, and his whole mind well balanced; but I do not suppose that any one would say that he possessed much original genius. He was deeply religious, and so orthodox that he told me one day he should be grieved if a single word of the Thirty-nine Articles were altered. His moral qualities were in every way admirable. He was free from every tinge of vanity or other petty feeling; and I never saw a man who thought so little about himself or his own concerns. His temper was imperturbably good, with the most winning and courteous manners; yet, as I have seen, he could be roused by any bad action to the warmest indignation and prompt action.

I once saw in his company in the streets of Cambridge almost as horrid a scene as could have been witnessed during the French Revolution. Two body snatchers had been arrested, and whilst being taken to prison had been torn from the constable by a crowd of the roughest men, who dragged them by their legs along the muddy and stony road. They were covered from head to foot with mud, and their faces were bleeding either from having been kicked or from the stones; they looked like corpses, but the crowd was so dense that I got only a few momentary glimpses of the wretched creatures. Never in my life have I seen such wrath painted on a man's face as was shown by Henslow at this horrid scene. He tried repeatedly to penetrate the mob; but it was simply impossible. He then rushed away to the mayor, telling me not to follow him, but to get more policemen. I forget the issue, except that the two men were got into the prison without being killed.

Henslow's benevolence was unbounded, as he proved by his many excellent schemes for his poor parishioners, when in after years he held the living of Hitcham. My intimacy with such a man ought to have been, and I hope was, an inestimable benefit. I cannot resist mentioning a trifling incident, which showed his kind consideration. Whilst examining some pollen-grains on a damp surface, I saw the tubes exserted, and instantly rushed off to communicate my surprising discovery to him. Now I do not suppose any other professor of botany could have helped laughing at my coming in such a hurry to make such a communication. But he agreed how interesting the phenomenon was, and explained its meaning, but made me clearly understand how well it was known; so I left him not in the least mortified, but well pleased at having discovered for myself so remarkable a fact, but determined not to be in such a hurry again to communicate my discoveries.

Dr. Whewell was one of the older and distinguished men who sometimes visited Henslow, and on several occasions I walked home with him at night. Next to Sir J. Mackintosh he was the best converser on grave subjects to whom I ever listened. Leonard Jenyns (The well-known Soame Jenyns was cousin to Mr. Jenyns' father.), who afterwards published some good essays in Natural History (Mr. Jenyns (now Blomefield) described the fish for the Zoology of the "Beagle"; and is author of a long series of papers, chiefly Zoological.), often stayed with Henslow, who was his brother-in-law. I visited him at his parsonage on the borders of the Fens [Swaffham Bulbeck], and had many a good walk and talk with him about Natural History. I became also acquainted with several other men older than me, who did not care much about science, but were friends of Henslow. One was a Scotchman, brother of Sir Alexander Ramsay, and tutor of Jesus College: he was a delightful man, but did not live for many years. Another was Mr. Dawes, afterwards Dean of Hereford, and famous for his success in the education of the poor. These men and others of the same standing, together with Henslow, used sometimes to take distant excursions into the country, which I was allowed to join, and they were most agreeable.

Looking back, I infer that there must have been something in me a little superior to the common run of youths, otherwise the above-mentioned men, so much older than me and higher in academical position, would never have allowed me to associate with them. Certainly I was not aware of any such superiority, and I remember one of my sporting friends, Turner, who saw me at work with my beetles, saying that I should some day be a Fellow of the Royal Society, and the notion seemed to me preposterous.

During my last year at Cambridge, I read with care and

profound interest Humboldt's "Personal Narrative." This work, and Sir J. Herschel's "Introduction to the Study of Natural Philosophy," stirred up in me a burning zeal to add even the most humble contribution to the noble structure of Natural Science. No one or a dozen other books influenced me nearly so much as these two. I copied out from Humboldt long passages about Teneriffe, and read them aloud on one of the above-mentioned excursions, to (I think) Henslow, Ramsay, and Dawes, for on a previous occasion I had talked about the glories of Teneriffe, and some of the party declared they would endeavour to go there; but I think that they were only half in earnest. I was, however, quite in earnest, and got an introduction to a merchant in London to enquire about ships; but the scheme was, of course, knocked on the head by the voyage of the "Beagle".

My summer vacations were given up to collecting beetles, to some reading, and short tours. In the autumn my whole time was devoted to shooting, chiefly at Woodhouse and Maer, and sometimes with young Eyton of Eyton. Upon the whole the three years which I spent at Cambridge were the most joyful in my happy life; for I was then in excellent health, and almost always in high spirits.

As I had at first come up to Cambridge at Christmas, I was forced to keep two terms after passing my final examination, at the commencement of 1831; and Henslow then persuaded me to begin the study of geology. Therefore on my return to Shropshire I examined sections, and coloured a map of parts round Shrewsbury. Professor Sedgwick intended to visit North Wales in the beginning of August to pursue his famous geological investigations amongst the older rocks, and Henslow asked him to allow me to accompany him. (In connection with this tour my father used to tell a story about Sedgwick: they had started from their inn one morning, and had walked a mile or two, when Sedgwick suddenly stopped, and vowed that he would return, being certain "that damned scoundrel" (the waiter) had not given the chambermaid the sixpence intrusted to him for the purpose. He was ultimately persuaded to give up the project, seeing that there was no reason for suspecting the waiter of especial perfidy.—F.D.) Accordingly he came and slept at my father's house.

A short conversation with him during this evening produced a strong impression on my mind. Whilst examining an old gravel-pit near Shrewsbury, a labourer told me that he had found in it a large worn tropical Volute shell, such as may be seen on the chimney-pieces of cottages; and as he would not sell the shell, I was convinced that he had really found it in the pit. I told Sedgwick of the fact, and he at once said (no doubt truly) that it must have been thrown away by some one into the pit; but then added, if really embedded there it would be the greatest misfortune to geology, as it would overthrow all that we know about the superficial deposits of the Midland Counties. These gravel-beds belong in fact to the glacial period, and in after years I found in them broken arctic shells. But I was then utterly astonished at Sedgwick not being delighted at so wonderful a fact as a tropical shell being found near the surface in the middle of England. Nothing before had ever made me thoroughly realise, though I had read various scientific books, that science consists in grouping facts so that general laws or conclusions may be drawn from them.

Next morning we started for Llangollen, Conway, Bangor, and Capel Curig. This tour was of decided use in teaching me a little how to make out the geology of a country.

Sedgwick often sent me on a line parallel to his, telling me to bring back specimens of the rocks and to mark the stratification on a map. I have little doubt that he did this for my good, as I was too ignorant to have aided him. On this tour I had a striking instance of how easy it is to overlook phenomena, however conspicuous, before they have been observed by any one. We spent many hours in Cwm Idwal, examining all the rocks with extreme care, as Sedgwick was anxious to find fossils in them; but neither of us saw a trace of the wonderful glacial phenomena all around us; we did not notice the plainly scored rocks, the perched boulders, the lateral and terminal moraines. Yet these phenomena are so conspicuous that, as I declared in a paper published many years afterwards in the "Philosophical Magazine" ("Philosophical Magazine," 1842.), a house burnt down by fire did not tell its story more plainly than did this valley. If it had still been filled by a glacier, the phenomena would have been less distinct than they now are.

At Capel Curig I left Sedgwick and went in a straight line by compass and map across the mountains to Barmouth, never following any track unless it coincided with my course. I thus came on some strange wild places, and enjoyed much this manner of travelling. I visited Barmouth to see some Cambridge friends who were reading there, and thence returned to Shrewsbury and to Maer for shooting; for at that time I should have thought myself mad to give up the first days of partridge-shooting for geology or any other science.

Chapter 3   Voyage of the "Beagle" from Dec. 27, 1831, to Oct. 2, 1836

On returning home from my short geological tour in North Wales, I found a letter from Henslow, informing me that Captain Fitz-Roy was willing to give up part of his own cabin to any young man who would volunteer to go with him without pay as naturalist to the Voyage of the "Beagle". I have given, as I believe, in my MS. Journal an account of all the circumstances which then occurred; I will here only say that I was instantly eager to accept the offer, but my father strongly objected, adding the words, fortunate for me,"If you can find any man of common sense who advises you to go I will give my consent." So I wrote that evening and refused the offer. On the next morning I went to Maer to be ready for September 1st, and, whilst out shooting, my uncle (Josiah Wedgwood.) sent for me, offering to drive me over to Shrewsbury and talk with my father, as my uncle thought it would be wise in me to accept the offer. My father always maintained that he was one of the most sensible men in the world, and he at once consented in the kindest manner. I had been rather extravagant at Cambridge, and to console my father, said, "that I should be deuced clever to spend more than my allowance whilst on board the 'Beagle'; " but he answered with a smile,"But they tell me you are very clever."

Next day I started for Cambridge to see Henslow, and thence to London to see Fitz-Roy, and all was soon arranged. Afterwards, on becoming very intimate with Fitz-Roy, I heard that I had run a very narrow risk of being rejected, on account of the shape of my nose! He was an ardent disciple of Lavater, and was convinced that he could judge of a man's character by the outline of his features; and he doubted whether any one with my nose could possess sufficient energy and determination for the voyage. But I think he was afterwards well satisfied that my nose had spoken falsely.

Fitz-Roy's character was a singular one, with very many noble features: he was devoted to his duty, generous to a fault, bold, determined, and indomitably energetic, and an ardent friend to all under his sway. He would undertake any sort of trouble to assist those whom he thought deserved assistance. He was a handsome man, strikingly like a gentleman, with highly courteous manners, which resembled those of his maternal uncle, the famous Lord Castlereagh, as I was told by the Minister at Rio. Nevertheless he must have inherited much in his appearance from Charles Ⅱ, for Dr. Wallich gave me a collection of photographs which he had made, and I was struck with the resemblance of one to Fitz-Roy; and on looking at the name, I found it Ch. E. Sobieski Stuart, Count d'Albanie, a descendant of the same monarch.

Fitz-Roy's temper was a most unfortunate one. It was usually worst in the early morning, and with his eagle eye he could generally detect something amiss about the ship, and was then unsparing in his blame. He was very kind to me, but was a man very difficult to live with on the intimate terms which necessarily followed from our messing by ourselves in the same cabin. We had several quarrels; for instance, early in the voyage at Bahia, in Brazil, he defended and praised slavery, which I abominated, and told me that he had just visited a great slave-owner, who had called up many of his slaves and asked them whether they were happy, and whether they wished to be free, and all answered "No." I then asked him, perhaps with a sneer, whether he thought that the answer of slaves in the presence of their master was worth anything? This made him excessively angry, and he said that as I doubted his word we could not live any longer together. I thought that I should have been compelled to leave the ship; but as soon as the news spread, which it did quickly, as the captain sent for the first lieutenant to assuage his anger by abusing me, I was deeply gratified by receiving an invitation from all the gun-room officers to mess with them. But after a few hours Fitz-Roy showed his usual magnanimity by sending an officer to me with an apology and a request that I would continue to live with him.

His character was in several respects one of the most noble which I have ever known.

The voyage of the "Beagle" has been by far the most important event in my life, and has determined my whole career; yet it depended on so small a circumstance as my uncle offering to drive me thirty miles to Shrewsbury, which few uncles would have done, and on such a trifle as the shape of my nose. I have always felt that I owe to the voyage the first real training or education of my mind; I was led to attend closely to several branches of natural history, and thus my powers of observation were improved, though they were always fairly developed.

The investigation of the geology of all the places visited was far more important, as reasoning here comes into play. On first examining a new district nothing can appear more hopeless than the chaos of rocks; but by recording the stratification and nature of the rocks and fossils at many points, always reasoning and predicting what will be found elsewhere, light soon begins to dawn on the district, and the structure of the whole becomes more or less intelligible. I had brought with me the first volume of Lyell's "Principles of Geology," which I studied attentively; and the book was of the highest service to me in many ways. The very first place which I examined, namely St. Jago in the Cape de Verde islands, showed me clearly the wonderful superiority of Lyell's manner of treating geology, compared with that of any other author, whose works I had with me or ever afterwards read.

Another of my occupations was collecting animals of all classes, briefly describing and roughly dissecting many of the marine ones; but from not being able to draw, and from not having sufficient anatomical knowledge, a great pile of MS. which I made during the voyage has proved almost useless. I thus lost much time, with the exception of that spent in acquiring some knowledge of the Crustaceans, as this was of service when in after years I undertook a monograph of the Cirripedia.

During some part of the day I wrote my Journal, and took much pains in describing carefully and vividly all that I had seen; and this was good practice. My Journal served also, in part, as letters to my home, and portions were sent to England whenever there was an opportunity.

The above various special studies were, however, of no importance compared with the habit of energetic industry and of concentrated attention to whatever I was engaged in, which I then acquired. Everything about which I thought or read was made to bear directly on what I had seen or was likely to see; and this habit of mind was continued during the five years of the voyage. I feel sure that it was this training which has enabled me to do whatever I have done in science.

Looking backwards, I can now perceive how my love for science gradually preponderated over every other taste. During the first two years my old passion for shooting survived in nearly full force, and I shot myself all the birds and animals for my collection; but gradually I gave up my gun more and more, and finally altogether, to my servant, as shooting interfered with my work, more especially with making out the geological structure of a country. I discovered, though unconsciously and insensibly, that the pleasure of observing and reasoning was a much higher one than that of skill and sport. That my mind became developed through my pursuits during the voyage is rendered probable by a remark made by my father, who was the most acute observer whom I ever saw, of a sceptical disposition, and far from being a believer in phrenology; for on first seeing me after the voyage, he turned round to my sisters, and exclaimed, "Why, the shape of his head is quite altered."

To return to the voyage. On September 11th (1831), I paid a flying visit with Fitz-Roy to the "Beagle" at Plymouth.

Thence to Shrewsbury to wish my father and sisters a long farewell. On October 24th I took up my residence at Plymouth, and remained there until December 27th, when the "Beagle" finally left the shores of England for her circumnavigation of the world. We made two earlier attempts to sail, but were driven back each time by heavy gales. These two months at Plymouth were the most miserable which I ever spent, though I exerted myself in various ways. I was out of spirits at the thought of leaving all my family and friends for so long a time, and the weather seemed to me inexpressibly gloomy. I was also troubled with palpitation and pain about the heart, and like many a young ignorant man, especially one with a smattering of medical knowledge, was convinced that I had heart disease. I did not consult any doctor, as I fully expected to hear the verdict that I was not fit for the voyage, and I was resolved to go at all hazards.

I need not here refer to the events of the voyage—where we went and what we did—as I have given a sufficiently full account in my published Journal. The glories of the vegetation of the Tropics rise before my mind at the present time more vividly than anything else; though the sense of sublimity, which the great deserts of Patagonia and the forest-clad mountains of Tierra del Fuego excited in me, has left an indelible impression on my mind. The sight of a naked savage in his native land is an event which can never be forgotten. Many of my excursions on horseback through wild countries, or in the boats, some of which lasted several weeks, were deeply interesting: their discomfort and some degree of danger were at that time hardly a drawback, and none at all afterwards. I also reflect with high satisfaction on some of my scientific work, such as solving the problem of coral islands, and making out the geological structure of certain islands, for instance, St. Helena. Nor must I pass over the discovery of the singular relations of the animals and plants inhabiting the several islands of the Galapagos archipelago, and of all of them to the inhabitants of South America.

As far as I can judge of myself, I worked to the utmost during the voyage from the mere pleasure of investigation, and from my strong desire to add a few facts to the great mass of facts in Natural Science. But I was also ambitious to take a fair place among scientific men,—whether more ambitious or less so than most of my fellow-workers, I can form no opinion.

The geology of St. Jago is very striking, yet simple: a stream of lava formerly flowed over the bed of the sea, formed of triturated recent shells and corals, which it has baked into a hard white rock. Since then the whole island has been upheaved. But the line of white rock revealed to me a new and important fact, namely, that there had been afterwards subsidence round the craters, which had since been in action, and had poured forth lava. It then first dawned on me that I might perhaps write a book on the geology of the various countries visited, and this made me thrill with delight. That was a memorable hour to me, and how distinctly I can call to mind the low cliff of lava beneath which I rested, with the sun glaring hot, a few strange desert plants growing near, and with living corals in the tidal pools at my feet. Later in the voyage, Fitz-Roy asked me to read some of my Journal, and declared it would be worth publishing; so here was a second book in prospect!

Towards the close of our voyage I received a letter whilst at Ascension, in which my sisters told me that Sedgwick had called on my father, and said that I should take a place among the leading scientific men. I could not at the time understand how he could have learnt anything of my proceedings, but I heard (I believe afterwards) that Henslow had read some of the letters which I wrote to him before the Philosophical Society of Cambridge (Read at the meeting held November 16, 1835, and printed in a pamphlet of 31 pages for distribution among the members of the Society.), and had printed them for private distribution. My collection of fossil bones, which had been sent to Henslow, also excited considerable attention amongst palaeontologists. After reading this letter, I clambered over the mountains of Ascension with a bounding step, and made the volcanic rocks resound under my geological hammer. All this shows how ambitious I was; but I think that I can say with truth that in after years, though I cared in the highest degree for the approbation of such men as Lyell and Hooker, who were my friends, I did not care much about the general public. I do not mean to say that a favourable review or a large sale of my books did not please me greatly, but the pleasure was a fleeting one, and I am sure that I have never turned one inch out of my course to gain fame.

Chapter 4   From My Return to England to My Marriage

These two years and three months were the most active ones which I ever spent, though I was occasionally unwell, and so lost some time. After going backwards and forwards several times between Shrewsbury, Maer, Cambridge, and London, I settled in lodgings at Cambridge (In Fitzwilliam Street.) on December 13th, where all my collections were under the care of Henslow. I stayed here three months, and got my minerals and rocks examined by the aid of Professor Miller.

I began preparing my "Journal of Travels," which was not hard work, as my MS. Journal had been written with care, and my chief labour was making an abstract of my more interesting scientific results. I sent also, at the request of Lyell, a short account of my observations on the elevation of the coast of Chile to the Geological Society. ("Geolog. Soc.

Proc." ii. 1838, pages 446-449.)

On March 7th, 1837, I took lodgings in Great Marlborough Street in London, and remained there for nearly two years, until I was married. During these two years I finished my Journal, read several papers before the Geological Society, began preparing the MS. for my "Geological Observations," and arranged for the publication of the "Zoology of the Voyage of the 'Beagle'." In July I opened my first note-book for facts in relation to the Origin of Species, about which I had long reflected, and never ceased working for the next twenty years.

During these two years I also went a little into society, and acted as one of the honorary secretaries of the Geological Society. I saw a great deal of Lyell. One of his chief characteristics was his sympathy with the work of others, and I was as much astonished as delighted at the interest which he showed when, on my return to England, I explained to him my views on coral reefs. This encouraged me greatly, and his advice and example had much influence on me. During this time I saw also a good deal of Robert Brown; I used often to call and sit with him during his breakfast on Sunday mornings, and he poured forth a rich treasure of curious observations and acute remarks, but they almost always related to minute points, and he never with me discussed large or general questions in science.

During these two years I took several short excursions as a relaxation, and one longer one to the Parallel Roads of Glen Roy, an account of which was published in the "Philosophical Transactions." (1839, pages 39-82.) This paper was a great failure, and I am ashamed of it. Having been deeply impressed with what I had seen of the elevation of the land of South America, I attributed the parallel lines to the action of the sea; but I had to give up this view when Agassiz propounded his glacier-lake theory. Because no other explanation was possible under our then state of knowledge, I argued in favour of sea-action; and my error has been a good lesson to me never to trust in science to the principle of exclusion.

As I was not able to work all day at science, I read a good deal during these two years on various subjects, including some metaphysical books; but I was not well fitted for such studies. About this time I took much delight in Wordsworth's and Coleridge's poetry; and can boast that I read the "Excursion" twice through. Formerly Milton's "Paradise Lost" had been my chief favourite, and in my excursions during the voyage of the "Beagle", when I could take only a single volume, I always chose Milton.

Chapter 5　From My Marriage, Jan. 29, 1839 to Settling at Down, Sept.14, 1842

(After speaking of his happy married life, and of his children, he continues: —)

During the three years and eight months whilst we resided in London, I did less scientific work, though I worked as hard as I possibly could, than during any other equal length of time in my life. This was owing to frequently recurring unwellness, and to one long and serious illness. The greater part of my time, when I could do anything, was devoted to my work on "Coral Reefs," which I had begun before my marriage, and of which the last proof-sheet was corrected on May 6th, 1842. This book, though a small one, cost me twenty months of hard work, as I had to read every work on the islands of the Pacific and to consult many charts. It was thought highly of by scientific men, and the theory therein given is, I think, now well established.

No other work of mine was begun in so deductive a spirit as this, for the whole theory was thought out on the west coast of South America, before I had seen a true coral reef. I had therefore only to verify and extend my views by a careful examination of living reefs. But it should be observed that I had during the two previous years been incessantly attending to the effects on the shores of South America of the intermittent elevation of the land, together with denudation and the deposition of sediment. This necessarily led me to reflect much on the effects of subsidence, and it was easy to replace in imagination the continued deposition of sediment by the upward growth of corals. To do this was to form my theory of the formation of barrier-reefs and atolls.

Besides my work on coral-reefs, during my residence in London, I read before the Geological Society papers on the Erratic Boulders of South America ("Geolog. Soc. Proc." iii. 1842.), on Earthquakes ("Geolog. Trans." v. 1840.), and on the Formation by the Agency of Earth-worms of Mould. ("Geolog. Soc. Proc." ii. 1838.) I also continued to superintend the publication of the "Zoology of the Voyage of the 'Beagle'." Nor did I ever intermit collecting facts bearing on the origin of species; and I could sometimes do this when I could do nothing else from illness.

In the summer of 1842 I was stronger than I had been for some time, and took a little tour by myself in North Wales, for the sake of observing the effects of the old glaciers which formerly filled all the larger valleys. I published a short account of what I saw in the "Philosophical Magazine." ("Philosophical Magazine," 1842.) This excursion interested me greatly, and it was the last time I was ever strong enough to climb mountains or to take long walks such as are necessary for geological work.

During the early part of our life in London, I was strong enough to go into general society, and saw a good deal of several scientific men, and other more or less distinguished men. I will give my impressions with respect to some of them, though I have little to say worth saying.

I saw more of Lyell than of any other man, both before and after my marriage. His mind was characterised, as it appeared to me, by clearness, caution, sound judgment, and a good deal of originality. When I made any remark to him on Geology, he never rested until he saw the whole case clearly, and often made me see it more clearly than I had done before. He would advance all possible objections to my suggestion, and even after these were exhausted would long remain dubious. A second characteristic was his hearty sympathy with the work of other scientific men. (The slight repetition here observable is accounted for by the notes on Lyell, etc., having been added in April, 1881, a few years after the rest of the "Recollections" were written.)

On my return from the voyage of the "Beagle", I explained to him my views on coral-reefs, which differed from his, and I was greatly surprised and encouraged by the vivid interest which he showed. His delight in science was ardent, and he felt the keenest interest in the future progress of mankind. He was very kind-hearted, and thoroughly liberal in his religious beliefs, or rather disbeliefs; but he was a strong theist. His candour was highly remarkable. He exhibited this by becoming a convert to the Descent theory, though he had gained much fame by opposing Lamarck's views, and this after he had grown old. He reminded me that I had many years before said to him, when discussing the opposition of the old school of geologists to his new views,"What a good thing it would be if every scientific man was to die when sixty years old, as afterwards he would be sure to oppose all new doctrines." But he hoped that now he might be allowed to live.

The science of Geology is enormously indebted to Lyell— more so, as I believe, than to any other man who ever lived. When [I was] starting on the voyage of the "Beagle", the sagacious Henslow, who, like all other geologists, believed at that time in successive cataclysms, advised me to get and study the first volume of the "Principles," which had then just been published, but on no account to accept the views therein advocated. How differently would anyone now speak of the "Principles"! I am proud to remember that the first place, namely, St. Jago, in the Cape de Verde archipelago, in which I geologised, convinced me of the infinite superiority of Lyell's views over those advocated in any other work known to me.

The powerful effects of Lyell's works could formerly be plainly seen in the different progress of the science in France and England. The present total oblivion of Elie de Beaumont's wild hypotheses, such as his "Craters of Elevation" and "Lines of Elevation" (which latter hypothesis I heard Sedgwick at the Geological Society lauding to the skies), may be largely attributed to Lyell.

I saw a good deal of Robert Brown,"facile Princeps Botanicorum," as he was called by Humboldt. He seemed to me to be chiefly remarkable for the minuteness of his observations, and their perfect accuracy. His knowledge was extraordinarily great, and much died with him, owing to his excessive fear of ever making a mistake. He poured out his knowledge to me in the most unreserved manner, yet was strangely jealous on some points. I called on him two or three times before the voyage of the "Beagle", and on one occasion he asked me to look through a microscope and describe what I saw. This I did, and believe now that it was the marvellous currents of protoplasm in some vegetable cell. I then asked him what I had seen; but he answered me,"That is my little secret."

He was capable of the most generous actions. When old, much out of health, and quite unfit for any exertion, he daily visited (as Hooker told me) an old man-servant, who lived at a distance (and whom he supported), and read aloud to him. This is enough to make up for any degree of scientific penuriousness or jealousy.

I may here mention a few other eminent men, whom I have occasionally seen, but I have little to say about them worth saying. I felt a high reverence for Sir J. Herschel, and was delighted to dine with him at his charming house at the Cape of Good Hope, and afterwards at his London house. I saw him, also, on a few other occasions. He never talked much, but every word which he uttered was worth listening to.

I once met at breakfast at Sir R. Murchison's house the illustrious Humboldt, who honoured me by expressing a wish to see me. I was a little disappointed with the great man, but my anticipations probably were too high. I can remember nothing distinctly about our interview, except that Humboldt was very cheerful and talked much.

— reminds me of Buckle whom I once met at Hensleigh Wedgwood's. I was very glad to learn from him his system of collecting facts. He told me that he bought all the books which he read, and made a full index, to each, of the facts which he thought might prove serviceable to him, and that he could always remember in what book he had read anything, for his memory was wonderful. I asked him how at first he could judge what facts would be serviceable, and he answered that he did not know, but that a sort of instinct guided him. From this habit of making indices, he was enabled to give the astonishing number of references on all sorts of subjects, which may be found in his "History of Civilisation." This book I thought most interesting, and read it twice, but I doubt whether his generalisations are worth anything. Buckle was a great talker, and I listened to him saying hardly a word, nor indeed could I have done so for he left no gaps. When Mrs. Farrer began to sing, I jumped up and said that I must listen to her; after I had moved away he turned around to a friend and said (as was overheard by my brother),"Well, Mr. Darwin's books are much better than his conversation."

Of other great literary men, I once met Sydney Smith at Dean Milman's house. There was something inexplicably amusing in every word which he uttered. Perhaps this was partly due to the expectation of being amused. He was talking about Lady Cork, who was then extremely old. This was the lady who, as he said, was once so much affected by one of his charity sermons, that she *borrowed* a guinea from a friend to put in the plate. He now said "It is generally believed that my dear old friend Lady Cork has been overlooked," and he said this in such a manner that no one could for a moment doubt that he meant that his dear old friend had been overlooked by the devil. How he managed to express this I know not.

I likewise once met Macaulay at Lord Stanhope's (the historian's) house, and as there was only one other man at dinner, I had a grand opportunity of hearing him converse, and he was very agreeable. He did not talk at all too much; nor indeed could such a man talk too much, as long as he allowed others to turn the stream of his conversation, and this he did allow.

Lord Stanhope once gave me a curious little proof of the accuracy and fulness of Macaulay's memory: many historians used often to meet at Lord Stanhope's house, and in discussing various subjects they would sometimes differ from Macaulay, and formerly they often referred to some book to see who was right; but latterly, as Lord Stanhope noticed, no historian ever took this trouble, and whatever Macaulay said was final.

On another occasion I met at Lord Stanhope's house, one of his parties of historians and other literary men, and amongst them were Motley and Grote. After luncheon I walked about Chevening Park for nearly an hour with Grote, and was much interested by his conversation and pleased by the simplicity and absence of all pretension in his manners.

Long ago I dined occasionally with the old Earl, the father of the historian; he was a strange man, but what little I knew of him I liked much. He was frank, genial, and pleasant. He had strongly marked features, with a brown complexion, and his clothes, when I saw him, were all brown. He seemed to believe in everything which was to others utterly incredible. He said one day to me,"Why don't you give up your fiddle-faddle of geology and zoology, and turn to the occult sciences!" The historian, then Lord Mahon, seemed shocked at such a speech to me, and his charming wife much amused.

The last man whom I will mention is Carlyle, seen by me several times at my brother's house, and two or three times at my own house. His talk was very racy and interesting, just like his writings, but he sometimes went on too long on the same subject. I remember a funny dinner at my brother's, where, amongst a few others, were Babbage and Lyell, both of whom liked to talk. Carlyle, however, silenced every one by haranguing during the whole dinner on the advantages of silence. After dinner Babbage, in his grimmest manner, thanked Carlyle for his very interesting lecture on silence.

Carlyle sneered at almost every one: one day in my house he called Grote's "History" "a fetid quagmire, with nothing spiritual about it." I always thought, until his "Reminiscences" appeared, that his sneers were partly jokes, but this now seems rather doubtful. His expression was that of a depressed, almost despondent yet benevolent man; and it is notorious how heartily he laughed. I believe that his benevolence was real, though stained by not a little jealousy. No one can doubt about his extraordinary power of drawing pictures of things and men—far more vivid, as it appears to me, than any drawn by Macaulay. Whether his pictures of men were true ones is another question.

He has been all-powerful in impressing some grand

moral truths on the minds of men. On the other hand, his views about slavery were revolting. In his eyes might was right. His mind seemed to me a very narrow one; even if all branches of science, which he despised, are excluded. It is astonishing to me that Kingsley should have spoken of him as a man well fitted to advance science. He laughed to scorn the idea that a mathematician, such as Whewell, could judge, as I maintained he could, of Goethe's views on light. He thought it a most ridiculous thing that any one should care whether a glacier moved a little quicker or a little slower, or moved at all. As far as I could judge, I never met a man with a mind so ill adapted for scientific research.

Whilst living in London, I attended as regularly as I could the meetings of several scientific societies, and acted as secretary to the Geological Society. But such attendance, and ordinary society, suited my health so badly that we resolved to live in the country, which we both preferred and have never repented of.

Chapter 6 Residence at Down from Sept. 14, 1842, to the Present Time, 1876

After several fruitless searches in Surrey and elsewhere, we found this house and purchased it. I was pleased with the diversified appearance of vegetation proper to a chalk district, and so unlike what I had been accustomed to in the Midland counties; and still more pleased with the extreme quietness and rusticity of the place. It is not, however, quite so retired a place as a writer in a German periodical makes it, who says that my house can be approached only by a mule-track! Our fixing ourselves here has answered admirably in one way, which we did not anticipate, namely, by being very convenient for frequent visits from our children.

Few persons can have lived a more retired life than we have done. Besides short visits to the houses of relations, and occasionally to the seaside or elsewhere, we have gone nowhere. During the first part of our residence we went a little into society, and received a few friends here; but my health almost always suffered from the excitement, violent shivering and vomiting attacks being thus brought on. I have therefore been compelled for many years to give up all dinner-parties; and this has been somewhat of a deprivation to me, as such parties always put me into high spirits. From the same cause I have been able to invite here very few scientific acquaintances.

My chief enjoyment and sole employment throughout life has been scientific work; and the excitement from such work makes me for the time forget, or drives quite away, my daily discomfort. I have therefore nothing to record during the rest of my life, except the publication of my several books. Perhaps a few details how they arose may be worth giving.

Chapter 7   My Several Publications

In the early part of 1844, my observations on the volcanic islands visited during the voyage of the"Beagle" were published. In 1845, I took much pains in correcting a new edition of my "Journal of Researches," which was originally published in 1839 as part of Fitz-Roy's work. The success of this, my first literary child, always tickles my vanity more than that of any of my other books. Even to this day it sells steadily in England and the United States, and has been translated for the second time into German, and into French and other languages. This success of a book of travels, especially of a scientific one, so many years after its first publication, is surprising. Ten thousand copies have been sold in England of the second edition. In 1846 my "Geological Observations on South America" were published. I record in a little diary, which I have always kept, that my three geological books ("Coral Reefs" included) consumed four and a half years' steady work;"and now it is ten years since my return to England. How much time have I lost by illness?" I have nothing to say about these three books except that to my surprise new editions have lately been called for. ("Geological Observations," 2nd Edit.1876. "Coral Reefs," 2nd Edit. 1874.)

In October, 1846, I began to work on "Cirripedia." When on the coast of Chile, I found a most curious form, which burrowed into the shells of Concholepas, and which differed so much from all other Cirripedes that I had to form a new sub-order for its sole reception. Lately an allied burrowing genus has been found on the shores of Portugal. To understand the structure of my new Cirripede I had to examine and dissect many of the common forms; and this gradually led me on to take up the whole group. I worked steadily on this subject for the next eight years, and ultimately published two thick volumes (Published by the Ray Society.), describing all the known living species, and two thin quartos on the extinct species. I do not doubt that Sir E. Lytton Bulwer had me in his mind when he introduced in one of his novels a Professor Long, who had written two huge volumes on limpets.

Although I was employed during eight years on this work, yet I record in my diary that about two years out of this time was lost by illness. On this account I went in 1848 for some months to Malvern for hydropathic treatment, which did me much good, so that on my return home I was able to resume work. So much was I out of health that when my dear father died on November 13th, 1848, I was unable to attend his funeral or to act as one of his executors.

My work on the Cirripedia possesses, I think, considerable value, as besides describing several new and remarkable forms, I made out the homologies of the various parts— I discovered the cementing apparatus, though I blundered dreadfully about the cement glands—and lastly I proved the existence in certain genera of minute males complemental to and parasitic on the hermaphrodites. This latter discovery has at last been fully confirmed; though at one time a German writer was pleased to attribute the whole account to my fertile imagination. The Cirripedes form a highly varying and difficult group of species to class; and my work was of considerable use to me, when I had to discuss in the

"Origin of Species" the principles of a natural classification. Nevertheless, I doubt whether the work was worth the consumption of so much time.

From September 1854 I devoted my whole time to arranging my huge pile of notes, to observing, and to experimenting in relation to the transmutation of species. During the voyage of the "Beagle" I had been deeply impressed by discovering in the Pampean formation great fossil animals covered with armour like that on the existing armadillos; secondly, by the manner in which closely allied animals replace one another in proceeding southwards over the Continent; and thirdly, by the South American character of most of the productions of the Galapagos archipelago, and more especially by the manner in which they differ slightly on each island of the group; none of the islands appearing to be very ancient in a geological sense.

It was evident that such facts as these, as well as many others, could only be explained on the supposition that species gradually become modified; and the subject haunted me. But it was equally evident that neither the action of the surrounding conditions, nor the will of the organisms (especially in the case of plants) could account for the innumerable cases in which organisms of every kind are beautifully adapted to their habits of life—for instance, a woodpecker or a tree-frog to climb trees, or a seed for dispersal by hooks or plumes. I had always been much struck by such adaptations, and until these could be explained it seemed to me almost useless to endeavour to prove by indirect evidence that species have been modified.

After my return to England it appeared to me that by following the example of Lyell in Geology, and by collecting all facts which bore in any way on the variation of animals and plants under domestication and nature, some light might perhaps be thrown on the whole subject. My first note-book was opened in July 1837. I worked on true Baconian principles, and without any theory collected facts on a wholesale scale, more especially with respect to domesticated productions, by printed enquiries, by conversation with skilful breeders and gardeners, and by extensive reading. When I see the list of books of all kinds which I read and abstracted, including whole series of Journals and Transactions, I am surprised at my industry.

I soon perceived that selection was the keystone of man's success in making useful races of animals and plants. But how selection could be applied to organisms living in a state of nature remained for some time a mystery to me.

In October 1838, that is, fifteen months after I had begun my systematic enquiry, I happened to read for amusement "Malthus on Population," and being well prepared to appreciate the struggle for existence which everywhere goes on from long-continued observation of the habits of animals and plants, it at once struck me that under these circumstances favourable variations would tend to be preserved, and unfavourable ones to be destroyed. The result of this would be the formation of new species. Here then I had at last got a theory by which to work; but I was so anxious to avoid prejudice, that I determined not for some time to write even the briefest sketch of it. In June 1842 I first allowed myself the satisfaction of writing a very brief abstract of my theory in pencil in 35 pages; and this was enlarged during the summer of 1844 into one of 230 pages, which I had fairly copied out and still possess.

But at that time I overlooked one problem of great

importance; and it is astonishing to me, except on the principle of Columbus and his egg, how I could have overlooked it and its solution. This problem is the tendency in organic beings descended from the same stock to diverge in character as they become modified. That they have diverged greatly is obvious from the manner in which species of all kinds can be classed under genera, genera under families, families under sub-orders and so forth; and I can remember the very spot in the road, whilst in my carriage, when to my joy the solution occurred to me; and this was long after I had come to Down. The solution, as I believe, is that the modified offspring of all dominant and increasing forms tend to become adapted to many and highly diversified places in the economy of nature.

Early in 1856 Lyell advised me to write out my views pretty fully, and I began at once to do so on a scale three or four times as extensive as that which was afterwards followed in my "Origin of Species;" yet it was only an abstract of the materials which I had collected, and I got through about half the work on this scale. But my plans were overthrown, for early in the summer of 1858 Mr.

Wallace, who was then in the Malay archipelago, sent me an essay "On the Tendency of Varieties to depart indefinitely from the Original Type;" and this essay contained exactly the same theory as mine. Mr. Wallace expressed the wish that if I thought well of his essay, I should sent it to Lyell for perusal.

The circumstances under which I consented at the request of Lyell and Hooker to allow of an abstract from my MS., together with a letter to Asa Gray, dated September 5, 1857, to be published at the same time with Wallace's Essay, are given in the "Journal of the Proceedings of the Linnean Society," 1858, page 45. I was at first very unwilling to consent, as I thought Mr. Wallace might consider my doing so unjustifiable, for I did not then know how generous and noble was his disposition. The extract from my MS. and the letter to Asa Gray had neither been intended for publication, and were badly written. Mr. Wallace's essay, on the other hand, was admirably expressed and quite clear. Nevertheless, our joint productions excited very little attention, and the only published notice of them which I can remember was by Professor Haughton of Dublin, whose verdict was that all that was new in them was false, and what was true was old. This shows how necessary it is that any new view should be explained at considerable length in order to arouse public attention.

In September 1858 I set to work by the strong advice of Lyell and Hooker to prepare a volume on the transmutation of species, but was often interrupted by ill-health, and short visits to Dr. Lane's delightful hydropathic establishment at Moor Park. I abstracted the MS. begun on a much larger scale in 1856, and completed the volume on the same reduced scale. It cost me thirteen months and ten days' hard labour. It was published under the title of the "Origin of Species," in November 1859. Though considerably added to and corrected in the later editions, it has remained substantially the same book.

It is no doubt the chief work of my life. It was from the first highly successful. The first small edition of 1250 copies was sold on the day of publication, and a second edition of 3000 copies soon afterwards. Sixteen thousand copies have now (1876) been sold in England; and considering how stiff a book it is, this is a large sale. It has been translated into almost every European tongue, even into such languages as Spanish, Bohemian, Polish, and Russian. It has also, according to Miss Bird, been translated into Japanese (Miss Bird is mistaken, as I learn from Prof. Mitsukuri.—F.D.), and is there much studied. Even an essay in Hebrew has appeared on it, showing that the theory is contained in the Old Testament! The reviews were very numerous; for some time I collected all that appeared on the "Origin" and on my related books, and these amount (excluding newspaper reviews) to 265; but after a time I gave up the attempt in despair. Many separate essays and books on the subject have appeared; and in Germany a catalogue or bibliography on "Darwinismus" has appeared every year or two.

The success of the "Origin" may, I think, be attributed in large part to my having long before written two condensed sketches, and to my having finally abstracted a much larger manuscript, which was itself an abstract. By this means I was enabled to select the more striking facts and conclusions. I had, also, during many years followed a golden rule, namely, that whenever a published fact, a new observation or thought came across me, which was opposed to my general results, to make a memorandum of it without fail and at once; for I had found by experience that such facts and thoughts were far more apt to escape from the memory than favourable ones. Owing to this habit, very few objections were raised against my views which I had not at least noticed and attempted to answer.

It has sometimes been said that the success of the "Origin" proved "that the subject was in the air," or "that men's minds were prepared for it." I do not think that this is strictly true, for I occasionally sounded not a few naturalists, and never happened to come across a single one who seemed to doubt about the permanence of species. Even Lyell and Hooker, though they would listen with interest to me, never seemed to agree. I tried once or twice to explain to able men what I meant by Natural Selection, but signally failed. What I believe was strictly true is that innumerable well-observed facts were stored in the minds of naturalists ready to take their proper places as soon as any theory which would receive them was sufficiently explained. Another element in the success of the book was its moderate size; and this I owe to the appearance of Mr. Wallace's essay; had I published on the scale in which I began to write in 1856, the book would have been four or five times as large as the "Origin," and very few would have had the patience to read it.

I gained much by my delay in publishing from about 1839, when the theory was clearly conceived, to 1859; and I lost nothing by it, for I cared very little whether men attributed most originality to me or Wallace; and his essay no doubt aided in the reception of the theory. I was forestalled in only one important point, which my vanity has always made me regret, namely, the explanation by means of the Glacial period of the presence of the same species of plants and of some few animals on distant mountain summits and in the arctic regions. This view pleased me so much that I wrote it out in extenso, and I believe that it was read by Hooker some years before E. Forbes published his celebrated memoir ("Geolog. Survey Mem.," 1846.) on the subject. In the very few points in which we differed, I still think that I was in the right. I have never, of course, alluded in print to my having independently worked out this view.

Hardly any point gave me so much satisfaction when I was at work on the "Origin," as the explanation of the wide difference in many classes between the embryo and the adult animal, and of the close resemblance of the embryos within the same class. No notice of this point was taken, as far as I remember, in the early reviews of the "Origin," and I recollect expressing my surprise on this head in a letter to Asa Gray. Within late years several reviewers have given the whole credit to Fritz Muller and Hackel, who undoubtedly have worked it out much more fully, and in some respects more correctly than I did. I had materials for a whole chapter on the subject, and I ought to have made the discussion longer; for it is clear that I failed to impress my readers; and he who succeeds in doing so deserves, in my opinion, all the credit.

This leads me to remark that I have almost always been treated honestly by my reviewers, passing over those without scientific knowledge as not worthy of notice. My views have often been grossly misrepresented, bitterly opposed and ridiculed, but this has been generally done, as I believe, in good faith. On the whole I do not doubt that my works have been over and over again greatly overpraised. I rejoice that I have avoided controversies, and this I owe to Lyell, who many years ago, in reference to my geological works, strongly advised me never to get entangled in a controversy, as it rarely did any good and caused a miserable loss of time and temper.

Whenever I have found out that I have blundered, or that my work has been imperfect, and when I have been contemptuously criticised, and even when I have been overpraised, so that I have felt mortified, it has been my greatest comfort to say hundreds of times to myself that "I have worked as hard and as well as I could, and no man can do more than this." I remember when in Good Success Bay, in Tierra del Fuego, thinking (and, I believe, that I wrote home to the effect) that I could not employ my life better than in adding a little to Natural Science. This I have done to the best of my abilities, and critics may say what they like, but they cannot destroy this conviction.

During the two last months of 1859 I was fully occupied in preparing a second edition of the "Origin," and by an enormous correspondence. On January 1st, 1860, I began arranging my notes for my work on the "Variation of Animals and Plants under Domestication;" but it was not published until the beginning of 1868; the delay having been caused partly by frequent illnesses, one of which lasted seven months, and partly by being tempted to publish on other subjects which at the time interested me more.

On May 15th, 1862, my little book on the "Fertilisation of Orchids," which cost me ten months' work, was published: most of the facts had been slowly accumulated during several previous years. During the summer of 1839, and, I believe, during the previous summer, I was led to attend to the cross-fertilisation of flowers by the aid of insects, from having come to the conclusion in my speculations on the origin of species, that crossing played an important part in keeping specific forms constant. I attended to the subject more or less during every subsequent summer; and my interest in it was greatly enhanced by having procured and read in November 1841, through the advice of Robert Brown, a copy of C.K. Sprengel's wonderful book, "Das entdeckte Geheimniss der Natur." For some years before 1862 I had specially attended to the fertilisation of our British orchids; and it seemed to me the best plan to prepare as complete a treatise on this group of plants as well as I could, rather than to utilise the great mass of matter which I had slowly collected with respect to other plants.

My resolve proved a wise one; for since the appearance of my book, a surprising number of papers and separate works on the fertilisation of all kinds of flowers have appeared: and these are far better done than I could possibly have effected. The merits of poor old Sprengel, so long overlooked, are now fully recognised many years after his death.

During the same year I published in the "Journal of the Linnean Society" a paper "On the Two Forms, or Dimorphic Condition of Primula," and during the next five years, five other papers on dimorphic and trimorphic plants. I do not think anything in my scientific life has given me so much satisfaction as making out the meaning of the structure of these plants. I had noticed in 1838 or 1839 the dimorphism of Linum flavum, and had at first thought that it was merely a case of unmeaning variability. But on examining the common species of Primula I found that the two forms were much too regular and constant to be thus viewed. I therefore became almost convinced that the common cowslip and primrose were on the high road to become dioecious;—that the short pistil in the one form, and the short stamens in the other form were tending towards abortion. The plants were therefore subjected under this point of view to trial; but as soon as the flowers with short pistils fertilised with pollen from the short stamens, were found to yield more seeds than any other of the four possible unions, the abortion-theory was knocked on the head. After some additional experiment, it became evident that the two forms, though both were perfect hermaphrodites, bore almost the same relation to one another as do the two sexes of an ordinary animal. With Lythrum we have the still more wonderful case of three forms standing in a similar relation to one another. I afterwards found that the offspring from the union of two plants belonging to the same forms presented a close and curious analogy with hybrids from the union of two distinct species.

In the autumn of 1864 I finished a long paper on "Climbing Plants," and sent it to the Linnean Society. The writing of this paper cost me four months; but I was so unwell when I received the proof-sheets that I was forced to leave them very badly and often obscurely expressed. The paper was little noticed, but when in 1875 it was corrected and published as a separate book it sold well. I was led to take up this subject by reading a short paper by Asa Gray, published in 1858. He sent me seeds, and on raising some plants I was so much fascinated and perplexed by the revolving movements of the tendrils and stems, which movements are really very simple, though appearing at first sight very complex, that I procured various other kinds of climbing plants, and studied the whole subject. I was all the more attracted to it, from not being at all satisfied with the explanation which Henslow gave us in his lectures, about twining plants, namely, that they had a natural tendency to grow up in a spire. This explanation proved quite erroneous. Some of the adaptations displayed by Climbing Plants are as beautiful as those of Orchids for ensuring cross-fertilisation.

My "Variation of Animals and Plants under Domestication" was begun, as already stated, in the beginning of 1860, but was not published until the beginning of 1868. It was a big book, and cost me four years and two months' hard labour. It gives all my observations and an immense number of facts collected from various sources, about our domestic productions. In the second volume the causes and laws of variation, inheritance, etc., are discussed as far as our present state of knowledge permits. Towards the end of the work I give my well-abused hypothesis of Pangenesis. An unverified hypothesis is of little or no value; but if anyone should hereafter be led to make observations by which some such hypothesis could be established, I shall have done good service, as an astonishing number of isolated facts can be thus connected together and rendered intelligible. In 1875 a second and largely corrected edition, which cost me a good deal of labour, was brought out.

My "Descent of Man" was published in February, 1871. As soon as I had become, in the year 1837 or 1838, convinced that species were mutable productions, I could not avoid the belief that man must come under the same law. Accordingly I collected notes on the subject for my own satisfaction, and not for a long time with any intention of publishing. Although in the "Origin of Species" the derivation of any particular species is never discussed, yet I thought it best, in order that no honourable man should accuse me of concealing my views, to add that by the work

"light would be thrown on the origin of man and his history."
It would have been useless and injurious to the success of
the book to have paraded, without giving any evidence, my
conviction with respect to his origin.

But when I found that many naturalists fully accepted
the doctrine of the evolution of species, it seemed to me
advisable to work up such notes as I possessed, and to
publish a special treatise on the origin of man. I was the
more glad to do so, as it gave me an opportunity of fully
discussing sexual selection— a subject which had always
greatly interested me. This subject, and that of the variation
of our domestic productions, together with the causes and
laws of variation, inheritance, and the intercrossing of plants,
are the sole subjects which I have been able to write about in
full, so as to use all the materials which I have collected. The
"Descent of Man" took me three years to write, but then as
usual some of this time was lost by ill health, and some was
consumed by preparing new editions and other minor works.
A second and largely corrected edition of the "Descent"
appeared in 1874.

My book on the "Expression of the Emotions in Men

and Animals" was published in the autumn of 1872. I had intended to give only a chapter on the subject in the "Descent of Man," but as soon as I began to put my notes together, I saw that it would require a separate treatise.

My first child was born on December 27th, 1839, and I at once commenced to make notes on the first dawn of the various expressions which he exhibited, for I felt convinced, even at this early period, that the most complex and fine shades of expression must all have had a gradual and natural origin. During the summer of the following year, 1840, I read Sir C. Bell's admirable work on expression, and this greatly increased the interest which I felt in the subject, though I could not at all agree with his belief that various muscles had been specially created for the sake of expression. From this time forward I occasionally attended to the subject, both with respect to man and our domesticated animals. My book sold largely; 5267 copies having been disposed of on the day of publication.

In the summer of 1860 I was idling and resting near Hartfield, where two species of Drosera abound; and I noticed that numerous insects had been entrapped by the leaves. I carried home some plants, and on giving them insects saw the movements of the tentacles, and this made me think it probable that the insects were caught for some special purpose. Fortunately a crucial test occurred to me, that of placing a large number of leaves in various nitrogenous and non-nitrogenous fluids of equal density; and as soon as I found that the former alone excited energetic movements, it was obvious that here was a fine new field for investigation.

During subsequent years, whenever I had leisure, I pursued my experiments, and my book on "Insectivorous Plants" was published in July 1875—that is, sixteen years after my first observations. The delay in this case, as with all my other books, has been a great advantage to me; for a man after a long interval can criticise his own work, almost as well as if it were that of another person. The fact that a plant should secrete, when properly excited, a fluid containing an acid and ferment, closely analogous to the digestive fluid of an animal, was certainly a remarkable discovery.

During this autumn of 1876 I shall publish on the "Effects of Cross and Self-Fertilisation in the Vegetable Kingdom."

This book will form a complement to that on the "Fertilisation of Orchids," in which I showed how perfect were the means for cross-fertilisation, and here I shall show how important are the results. I was led to make, during eleven years, the numerous experiments recorded in this volume, by a mere accidental observation; and indeed it required the accident to be repeated before my attention was thoroughly aroused to the remarkable fact that seedlings of self-fertilised parentage are inferior, even in the first generation, in height and vigour to seedlings of cross-fertilised parentage. I hope also to republish a revised edition of my book on Orchids, and hereafter my papers on dimorphic and trimorphic plants, together with some additional observations on allied points which I never have had time to arrange. My strength will then probably be exhausted, and I shall be ready to exclaim "Nunc dimittis."

Chapter 8   Written May 1st, 1881

"The Effects of Cross and Self-Fertilisation" was published in the autumn of 1876; and the results there arrived at explain, as I believe, the endless and wonderful contrivances for the transportal of pollen from one plant to another of the same species. I now believe, however, chiefly from the observations of Hermann Muller, that I ought to have insisted more strongly than I did on the many adaptations for self-fertilisation; though I was well aware of many such adaptations. A much enlarged edition of my "Fertilisation of Orchids" was published in 1877.

In this same year "The Different Forms of Flowers, etc.," appeared, and in 1880 a second edition. This book consists chiefly of the several papers on Heterostyled flowers originally published by the Linnean Society, corrected, with much new matter added, together with observations on some other cases in which the same plant bears two kinds of flowers. As before remarked, no little discovery of mine ever gave me so much pleasure as the making out the meaning of heterostyled flowers. The results of crossing such flowers in an illegitimate manner, I believe to be very important, as bearing on the sterility of hybrids; although these results have been noticed by only a few persons.

In 1879, I had a translation of Dr. Ernst Krause's "Life of Erasmus Darwin" published, and I added a sketch of his character and habits from material in my possession. Many persons have been much interested by this little life, and I am surprised that only 800 or 900 copies were sold.

In 1880 I published, with [my son] Frank's assistance, our "Power of Movement in Plants." This was a tough piece of work. The book bears somewhat the same relation to my little book on "Climbing Plants," which "Cross-Fertilisation" did to the "Fertilisation of Orchids;" for in accordance with the principle of evolution it was impossible to account for climbing plants having been developed in so many widely different groups unless all kinds of plants possess some slight power of movement of an analogous kind. This I proved to be the case; and I was further led to a rather wide generalisation, viz. that the great and important classes of movements, excited by light, the attraction of gravity, etc., are all modified forms of the fundamental movement of circumnutation. It has always pleased me to exalt plants in the scale of organised beings; and I therefore felt an especial pleasure in showing how many and what admirably well adapted movements the tip of a root possesses.

I have now (May 1, 1881) sent to the printers the MS. of a little book on "The Formation of Vegetable Mould, through the Action of Worms." This is a subject of but small importance; and I know not whether it will interest any readers (Between November 1881 and February 1884, 8500 copies have been sold.), but it has interested me. It is the completion of a short paper read before the Geological Society more than forty years ago, and has revived old geological thoughts.

I have now mentioned all the books which I have published, and these have been the milestones in my life, so that little remains to be said. I am not conscious of any change in my mind during the last thirty years, excepting in one point presently to be mentioned; nor, indeed, could any change have been expected unless one of general deterioration. But my father lived to his eighty-third year with his mind as lively as ever it was, and all his faculties undimmed; and I hope that I may die before my mind fails to a sensible extent. I think that I have become a little more skilful in guessing right explanations and in devising experimental tests; but this may probably be the result of mere practice, and of a larger store of knowledge. I have as much difficulty as ever in expressing myself clearly and concisely; and this difficulty has caused me a very great loss of time; but it has had the compensating advantage of forcing me to think long and intently about every sentence, and thus I have been led to see errors in reasoning and in my own observations or those of others.

There seems to be a sort of fatality in my mind leading me to put at first my statement or proposition in a wrong or awkward form. Formerly I used to think about my sentences before writing them down; but for several years I have found that it saves time to scribble in a vile hand whole pages as quickly as I possibly can, contracting half the words; and then correct deliberately. Sentences thus scribbled down are often better ones than I could have written deliberately.

Having said thus much about my manner of writing, I will add that with my large books I spend a good deal of time over the general arrangement of the matter. I first make the rudest outline in two or three pages, and then a larger one in several pages, a few words or one word standing for a whole discussion or series of facts. Each one of these headings is again enlarged and often transferred before I begin to write in extenso. As in several of my books facts observed by others have been very extensively used, and as I have always had several quite distinct subjects in hand at the same time, I may mention that I keep from thirty to forty large portfolios, in cabinets with labelled shelves, into which I can at once put a detached reference or memorandum. I have bought many books, and at their ends I make an index of all the facts that concern my work; or, if the book is not my own, write out a separate abstract, and of such abstracts I have a large drawer full. Before beginning on any subject I look to all the short indexes and make a general and classified index, and by taking the one or more proper portfolios I have all the information collected during my life ready for use.

I have said that in one respect my mind has changed during the last twenty or thirty years. Up to the age of thirty, or beyond it, poetry of many kinds, such as the works of Milton, Gray, Byron, Wordsworth, Coleridge, and Shelley, gave me great pleasure, and even as a schoolboy I took intense delight in Shakespeare, especially in the historical plays. I have also said that formerly pictures gave me considerable, and music very great delight. But now for many years I cannot endure to read a line of poetry: I have tried lately to read Shakespeare, and found it so intolerably dull that it nauseated me. I have also almost lost my taste for pictures or music. Music generally sets me thinking too energetically on what I have been at work on, instead of giving me pleasure. I retain some taste for fine scenery, but it does not cause me the exquisite delight which it formerly did. On the other hand, novels which are works of the imagination, though not of a very high order, have been for years a wonderful relief and pleasure to me, and I often bless all novelists. A surprising number have been read aloud to me, and I like all if moderately good, and if they do not end unhappily — against which a law ought to be passed. A novel, according to my taste, does not come into the first class unless it contains some person whom one can thoroughly love, and if a pretty woman all the better.

This curious and lamentable loss of the higher aesthetic tastes is all the odder, as books on history, biographies, and travels (independently of any scientific facts which they may contain), and essays on all sorts of subjects interest me as much as ever they did. My mind seems to have become a kind of machine for grinding general laws out of large collections of facts, but why this should have caused the atrophy of that part of the brain alone, on which the higher tastes depend, I cannot conceive. A man with a mind more highly organised or better constituted than mine, would not, I suppose, have thus suffered; and if I had to live my life again, I would have made a rule to read some poetry and listen to some music at least once every week; for perhaps the parts of my brain now atrophied would thus have been kept active through use. The loss of these tastes is a loss of happiness, and may possibly be injurious to the intellect, and more probably to the moral character, by enfeebling the emotional part of our nature.

My books have sold largely in England, have been translated into many languages, and passed through several editions in foreign countries. I have heard it said that the success of a work abroad is the best test of its enduring value. I doubt whether this is at all trustworthy; but judged by this standard my name ought to last for a few years. Therefore it may be worth while to try to analyse the mental qualities and the conditions on which my success has depended; though I am aware that no man can do this correctly.

I have no great quickness of apprehension or wit which is so remarkable in some clever men, for instance, Huxley. I am therefore a poor critic: a paper or book, when first read, generally excites my admiration, and it is only after considerable reflection that I perceive the weak points. My power to follow a long and purely abstract train of thought is very limited; and therefore I could never have succeeded with metaphysics or mathematics. My memory is extensive, yet hazy: it suffices to make me cautious by vaguely telling me that I have observed or read something opposed to the conclusion which I am drawing, or on the other hand in favour of it; and after a time I can generally recollect where to search for my authority. So poor in one sense is my memory, that I have never been able to remember for more than a few days a single date or a line of poetry.

Some of my critics have said, "Oh, he is a good observer, but he has no power of reasoning!" I do not think that this can be true, for the "Origin of Species" is one long argument from the beginning to the end, and it has convinced not a few able men. No one could have written it without having some power of reasoning. I have a fair share of invention, and of common sense or judgment, such as every fairly successful lawyer or doctor must have, but not, I believe, in any higher degree.

On the favourable side of the balance, I think that I am superior to the common run of men in noticing things which easily escape attention, and in observing them carefully. My industry has been nearly as great as it could have been in the observation and collection of facts. What is far more important, my love of natural science has been steady and ardent.

This pure love has, however, been much aided by the ambition to be esteemed by my fellow naturalists. From my early youth I have had the strongest desire to understand or explain whatever I observed,—that is, to group all facts under some general laws. These causes combined have given me the patience to reflect or ponder for any number of years over any unexplained problem. As far as I can judge, I am not apt to follow blindly the lead of other men. I have steadily endeavoured to keep my mind free so as to give up any hypothesis, however much beloved (and I cannot resist forming one on every subject), as soon as facts are shown to be opposed to it. Indeed, I have had no choice but to act in this manner, for with the exception of the Coral Reefs, I cannot remember a single first-formed hypothesis which had not after a time to be given up or greatly modified. This has naturally led me to distrust greatly deductive reasoning in the mixed sciences. On the other hand, I am not very sceptical,—a frame of mind which I believe to be injurious to the progress of science. A good deal of scepticism in a scientific man is advisable to avoid much loss of time, but I have met with not a few men, who, I feel sure, have often thus been deterred from experiment or observations, which would have proved directly or indirectly serviceable.

In illustration, I will give the oddest case which I have known. A gentleman (who, as I afterwards heard, is a good local botanist) wrote to me from the Eastern counties that the seed or beans of the common field-bean had this year everywhere grown on the wrong side of the pod. I wrote back, asking for further information, as I did not understand what was meant; but I did not receive any answer for a very long time. I then saw in two newspapers, one published in Kent and the other in Yorkshire, paragraphs stating that it was a most remarkable fact that "the beans this year had all grown on the wrong side." So I thought there must be some foundation for so general a statement. Accordingly, I went to my gardener, an old Kentish man, and asked him whether he had heard anything about it, and he answered,"Oh, no, sir, it must be a mistake, for the beans grow on the wrong side only on leap-year, and this is not leap-year." I then asked him how they grew in common years and how on leap-years, but soon found that he knew absolutely nothing of how they grew at any time, but he stuck to his belief.

After a time I heard from my first informant, who, with many apologies, said that he should not have written to me had he not heard the statement from several intelligent farmers; but that he had since spoken again to every one of them, and not one knew in the least what he had himself meant. So that here a belief—if indeed a statement with no definite idea attached to it can be called a belief—had spread over almost the whole of England without any vestige of evidence.

I have known in the course of my life only three intentionally falsified statements, and one of these may have been a hoax (and there have been several scientific hoaxes) which, however, took in an American Agricultural Journal. It related to the formation in Holland of a new breed of oxen by the crossing of distinct species of Bos (some of which I happen to know are sterile together), and the author had the impudence to state that he had corresponded with me, and that I had been deeply impressed with the importance of his result. The article was sent to me by the editor of an English Agricultural Journal, asking for my opinion before republishing it.

A second case was an account of several varieties, raised

by the author from several species of Primula, which had spontaneously yielded a full complement of seed, although the parent plants had been carefully protected from the access of insects. This account was published before I had discovered the meaning of heterostylism, and the whole statement must have been fraudulent, or there was neglect in excluding insects so gross as to be scarcely credible.

The third case was more curious: Mr. Huth published in his book on "Consanguineous Marriage" some long extracts from a Belgian author, who stated that he had interbred rabbits in the closest manner for very many generations, without the least injurious effects. The account was published in a most respectable Journal, that of the Royal Society of Belgium; but I could not avoid feeling doubts—I hardly know why, except that there were no accidents of any kind, and my experience in breeding animals made me think this very improbable.

So with much hesitation I wrote to Professor Van Beneden, asking him whether the author was a trustworthy man. I soon heard in answer that the Society had been greatly shocked by discovering that the whole account was a fraud. (The falseness of the published statements on which Mr. Huth relied has been pointed out by himself in a slip inserted in all the copies of his book which then remained unsold.) The writer had been publicly challenged in the Journal to say where he had resided and kept his large stock of rabbits while carrying on his experiments, which must have consumed several years, and no answer could be extracted from him.

My habits are methodical, and this has been of not a little use for my particular line of work. Lastly, I have had ample leisure from not having to earn my own bread. Even ill-health, though it has annihilated several years of my life, has saved me from the distractions of society and amusement.

Therefore my success as a man of science, whatever this may have amounted to, has been determined, as far as I can judge, by complex and diversified mental qualities and conditions. Of these, the most important have been—the love of science—unbounded patience in long reflecting over any subject—industry in observing and collecting facts—and a fair share of invention as well as of common sense. With such moderate abilities as I possess, it is truly surprising that I should have influenced to a considerable extent the belief of scientific men on some important points.